Contents

	Note from the Author	4
	Dedication	5
	Preface	6
	Introduction	10
1	Getting Started	13
2	Your First Calls	28
3	More Forms You Need	37
4	Telephone Inquiries	49
5	Veterinarian Release Form	53
6	The Interview	57
7	Doing the Job, Step by Step	74
8	Finishing Touches	85
9	Supplementary Sales Ideas	91
10	Bird Boarding	106
11	Keeping Your Ducks in a Row	113
12	Accounts Receivable	122
13	Was Your Year End a Success?	127
14	Insurance—Do You Need It?	131
15	What's in a Name?	136
16	Cardholders and Doughnuts	141
17	Why Have all the Answers?	145
18	A Formal Presentation Book	148
19	Odds and Ends	153
20	What is the Best?	171

Note from the Author

This book is primarily a book of practices and principles which will apply to the same circumstances in Canada as in the United States. However, since I do live in Los Angeles, California, my instructions as to three specific United States requirements for business may be different for Canada. The three items are:

business license
false name filing
false name statement.

Pricing, likewise, may be different dependent upon the city in which you decide to open your business. This is not to say the principles by which you determine your pricing won't work, just that due to our differing dollar rates your pricing should be guided accordingly.

The tax liability of your business may also differ from the United States laws. Our laws for taxation, like yours, continue to change yearly. For example, in 1989 the U.S. deduction for telephone expense for business was changed to allow deduction only if the owner possessed a separate line for business and a separate line for personal telephone service; prior to that, business expense calls were deductible on a single line. It is a wise idea to check with a good tax book or a reputable accountant prior to making any claim for tax deduction on items that may have been considered "standard" in either of our countries in the past.

All the other principles upon which this book is based remain the same. My company, *Paw Partners,* is run no differently from your company. People with pets are the same all over the world. We all want our pets to have tender, loving, professional care.

Good fortune,
Bill Foster

Starting a Pet Sitting Business

By William S. Foster

Illustrated by Rubén Cueto

ISBN 0-88839-241-9
Copyright © 1990 William Steven Foster

Cataloging in Publication Data
Foster, William S. (William Steven), 1941-
   Starting a pet sitting business

   ISBN 0-88839-241-9

   1. Pet sitting.   I. Title.

   SF414.34.F67 1990   636.088'7'023   C90-091106-9

All rights reserved. No part of this publication may be reproduced, stored in a retrieval system or transmitted, in any form or by any means, electronic, mechanical, photocopying, recording or otherwise, without the prior written permission of Hancock House Publishers.

Cover and Illustrations by Reubén Cueto
Editing, Typesetting, and Production by Cheryl Smiley
Production by Lorna Lake
Senior Editor and Design by Herb Bryce

Printed in Hong Kong

Published simultaneously in Canada and the United States by

HANCOCK HOUSE PUBLISHERS LTD.
19313 Zero Avenue, Surrey, B.C. V3S 5J9

HANCOCK HOUSE PUBLISHERS
1431 Harrison Avenue, P. O. Box X-1, Blaine, WA 98230

Dedication

This book is respectfully dedicated to our clients. Thanks to the continued support of our pet friends, this experience called pet sitting has been possible. You are all beautiful.

Abbie, Abby, Acana, Ajax, Amberino Snow, Amy, Andora, Apollo, Archibald, B.G., Baby, Bailey, Bardot, Barnum, Bear, Beau, Beng, Bert, Biko, Billy Joe, Blondie, Bogart, Boof, Boomer, Brandy, Bridget, Bruiser, Buckwheat, Buddy, Butterball, Buttercup, C.J., Cactus Claws, Cadbury Bissonette, Cale, Calliope, Cally, Cat, Champagne, Changa, Chani, Chanti, Chanton, Charlie, Charlie Chan Too, Cheeky, Chester, China Doll, Chloe, Cindy, Cindy-Spot, Cinnamon, Circles, Cleo, Clyde, Coal, Coco, Cookie, Cricket, Curry, Cynabar, Daisy, Dakota, Dee Jay, Dewey, Digger, Dudette, Dudette II, Dudley, Duffy, Dumpy, Duncan, Dusty, Dusty Cole Bynn, Eberly, Elvira, Empress, Ethel, Fancy, Fatty, Fluffy, Frances, Fred, Friday, Fritz, Gato, Ginger, Goliath, Gracie, Guy, Harriett, Heidi, Hogan, Holly, Hoosh, Iron Man, Issac, J.R., Jack, Jacque, Jake, Jasmine, Jasper, Jelly Bean, Jenny, Jessica, Jet, Joey, Johnny, Juice, Kallu, Kate, Keeters, Kelly, Kichu, Kidd, Kimba, Kitty, Kodi, Krystle, Kula, Lady, Lady Cat, Lars, Lasha, Leo, Lizabeth, Lizzie, Louis, Lucy, Luiji, Lupe, Maggie, Mai-Tai, Major, Mandy, Mariah, Marquey, Mattie, Max, Mayday, Mikka, Mimi, Misha, Mister Wiggles, Molly, Monroe, Mopsey, Morgan, Mouse, Murphy Brown, Nako, Napoleon, Natasha, Nicholaus, Nick, Nijinsky, Niki, Nuke, Ohno, Ollie, Packy, Paco, Pandy, Peaches, Peanut, Pearl, Pepper, Pepsi, Phil, Piper, Pippin, Pistol, Pluto, Prancer, Princess, Prissy, Puck, Puff, Pyewacket, Rags, Raleigh, Ralph, Rebel, Remy, Rex, Rocky, Roger, Rudy, Sabrina, Sadie, Salt, Sam, Samantha, Sambo, Sandi, Schoen, Scuzzy, Seymour, Shadow, Shannon, Sharu, Shogun, Sidney, Simon, Skipper, Smokey, Smokie, Smudge, Snooks, Snoopy, Snow, Sophie, Spats, Spike, Spooky, Spot, Squeeki, Stacy, Stanley, Suki, Summer, Tabitha, Taffy, Tammie, Tasha, Tawny, Taz, Teddy, Terra, Tia, Tiger, Tinker, Tip-Sing, Toby, Tomak, Tony Tiger, Toughey, Truffles, Tuffy, Tugar, Turtle, Usagi, Violet, Westin, Wheezy, William, Willie, Wong, Woodstock, You Guy, Ziggy, Zorba.

And dozens and dozens of assorted stray cats!

Preface

The preface usually contains a scroll of thank yous to all the people who make the book possible. This won't. I have only my clients to thank for my business, the pet industry people for being a fountain of information, my own pets for giving me ample practice, and my wife for being my rock for the past twenty years.

The same dream kept drifting into my head, over and over again. Wouldn't it be nice to wake up each morning before the alarm clock went off? Wake up eager to get out of bed and ready to start the new day? Wouldn't it be nice to go to work filled with enthusiasm, anticipation, and excitement at what the new day might hold? It was a nice dream, but it never happened. Never happened, that is, until now.

I've always had to work. There lies the key phrase, "had to work." Not eager to work. Not work that I loved and was truly interested in, but simply a means to obtain a paycheck. Like most people, I daydreamed about owning my own business. I thought about various enterprises in which I could use my skills. The only trouble was that those thoughts kept coming back to one big problem: lack of money!

You start out in an occupation sometimes by accident, sometimes by plan, but you end up using the skills you learn over and over again. I kept remembering the words of my father: "Son, as long as you work for the man who writes the paycheck, you'll never, ever, get rich." My father was a successful entrepreneur who worked for himself his entire lifetime. He was right. Your ultimate destiny is controlled by that person who writes out that check for you every single month. Just to keep that paycheck coming in, I traveled the entire United States. Every week I got home exhausted on Saturday morning and left again on Sunday evening.

In the life I now lead, my time is my own. I do what I want, when I want, where I want. I write my own paycheck. I am in charge of my own destiny. I decide what is important to me, and what is not.

Many how-to books or success books are written backwards. A successful entrepreneur is approached and asked to write a book on how that person became successful. The business owner sits down, thinks for a long while, and tries to decide what formula would make a good story or interesting reading. This book was written forwards. I began keeping notes the day I went into business and worked forward, through each day, week, and month, until I ended up with a formula that truly reflects what I actually did, not just what makes a good story.

Although this book is about my business of pet sitting, the formula for starting a service business has applications which are much, much broader. You can use this same method, these same forms, to establish yourself in businesses such as:

lawn care
window cleaning
chauffeuring
personal shopping
aquarium maintenance
house sitting
pool maintenance
delivery service.

Any business which falls under the heading of personal service can utilize the principles put forward in this book.

The question I am most frequently asked is "How did you get into this business in the first place?" Here's the true story.

It was early November and Thanksgiving weekend was looming. My wife and I always look forward to going out of town over the holidays and relaxing. We own three poodles and they are our children. Our poodles have a doggie door and a fenced backyard. I wanted somebody to come visit my house, bring in my mail, pick up the paper, change the lights, water the houseplants, feed the dogs, and generally make certain everything was looked after.

I began calling around to pet shops and veterinarians, asking where I could find such a person. I wanted someone reliable, trustworthy, honest, punctual, and above all, someone who would take good care of my pets. I never found that person. After about eight calls, I gave up in disgust and said to my wife, "Why doesn't somebody go into this business? There is obviously a big need here." My wife turned to me with a wry grin and said, "If you're so smart, why don't you do it?" I mulled the idea over for a week and then took out an application for my business license.

In some types of business they tell you that if you survive the first two years, then you will begin to make a living. I made money from the very first week I installed my answering machine! I have never had a month since then that I didn't make money.

There are basic principles in this book that make any service-related business work. They are repeated throughout the book in almost every chapter. Every single time I made a mistake (and I made plenty of them), I asked myself this question, "How could I have done that correctly?" I tried to think of alternatives and then, the next time, I would try something new. When something finally worked properly, I would discard the old method and insert the new one. You will find the ideas that fill this book work all the time. I use them daily, on a routine basis. That is why I am successful in my business. You will be successful in your business, too, using the same methods!

The biggest secret to becoming self-employed is keep your operation simple. This cannot be overstated. You are not starting out to be IBM or General Motors; you just want a small, easy-to-run business, which follows the dictates of your own personality. Even if you have sufficient funds to establish an elaborate, complex business, you will soon find that the business is running you, not the other way around.

The second biggest secret is in being the very best at what you do. Leave absolutely no doubt whatsoever that when any customer hires you, that person is getting the very best person available anywhere. The idea of being the best is going to become a trend once again. Personal service has come full circle. In the forties and fifties America was the best. My reason for wanting to be the very best is not only the result of personal pride, but it is also caused by my aggravation and exasperation in dealing with other service businesses.

Unfortunately, you are surrounded by carelessness every day. Full service gas stations where attendants don't check the oil unless badgered; banks which spend thousands of dollars on advertising to get you in the door and then don't open a window to serve you quickly; the post office has expensive ads on television proclaiming absolute overnight delivery and then the clerk at the local office tells you, "only in a limited area." The list goes on and on.

The standards of service in America have become so poor that my first-time customers are actually shocked when everything is done correctly! Isn't that sad? My customers thank me profusely for doing such a good job because my customers are used to settling for poor service. I consider it my duty to perform to a high standard; but most people are being forced to settle for mediocrity. I guarantee you that it is easy for you to be the best because your competition is ill-prepared, unprofessional, and careless. Doing your absolute best not only gets you compliments, but also reaps monetary rewards. My repeat customer level, at present, is approaching 80 percent. I charge more money than most of my competitors anywhere in Los Angeles. So why do people spend more money for me? Service. Good, reliable service.

Until now, almost all of my customers have wrongly assumed that no real money could be made in my business. I was just a person they were lucky enough to find for a sitter. I never discuss income opportunities with my customers because if they want to feel sorry for me, that's fine.

The simple format outlined in this book is designed to save you time, mistakes, money, and effort.

Introduction

The most successful entrepreneurial enterprise is one that does not involve a product. Instead, it sells a service. This allows for minimal overhead and extremely low expenses. This is why the field of pet sitting is ideal for anyone interested in high income and low overhead. As I will show you in this book, your total cash outlay prior to getting into business can be less than $300. Once in business, your maximum costs are still less than $500 a month, even during peak income months. What business can you imagine where you could be self-employed within three days on less than $300? My first customer booking started only two days after I began my business. Yours can too! By the seventh working day I had booked over $400 worth of business. You can too! In the first two weeks I had more than twenty-one telephone calls about my business. You can too!

This book is outlined in a logical, sequential, step-by-step manner which is mandatory for your success. If you leave out any of these steps, you jeopardize your maximum income potential. Please read and reread the entire book prior to beginning any phase of your operation. Don't approach self-employment carelessly. Don't read directions when all else fails. Because then you will fail. I learned by trial and error; you don't have to do that. Profit from my mistakes and my acquired knowledge.

Like any business in which promotion is involved, you are selling a service. More important than the service, you are selling yourself. Your honesty, your enthusiasm, your integrity, your dependability, and your credibility are what the customer must accept before you get that first appointment, let alone the first job. You must first determine how much time, effort, and commitment you are willing to put into this project. The income will roll into your hands as a natural by-product of your good service.

Never concentrate on money alone as your main goal. That may sound odd to you since money (income) is the main goal in any occupation. If you concentrate on money alone, however, you will fail in your ultimate goal. Instead of money, think about helping your customers. You are providing a service that only you can provide.

You are going to make the customer's vacation a success.
You are going to eliminate worry while your customer is gone.
You are going to make certain the customer's home is secure.
You are going to maintain the pet's health.
You are going to feed, love, and play with the pets.
You are going to take care of the mail.
You are going to bring in the newspapers.
You are going to water the houseplants.
You are going to let the customer know what happened during their absence.
You are going to become a vital part of the customer's life.
You are going to be richly rewarded for your efforts.

If you have access to a car, and are in reasonably good health, you already possess nine-tenths of all the tools you will need. The basic ingredient that needs to be added now is time, your time. You will find that your time is going to be worth money. This is not to be confused with something for nothing. You are going to have to work for your money. You may well book thousands of dollars in the first weeks and months, but you are going to have to fulfill those obligations in order to get paid. Nobody in this world gets something for nothing. This is the best of all possible service industries because what you are giving to the customer is highly visible, easily recognizable, and in high demand regardless of where you live.

If you happen to live in an area of the United States, such as Los Angeles, where the price of land is increasing in value by double-digit percentages, you will find that kennels and boarding facilities are closing as the land becomes commercially viable to develop for other uses. Zoning commissions are making rulings on a regular basis that exclude boarding facilities from the confines of many cities. This pushes the boarding services further and further out of town, and makes the facility harder for the customer to reach. It also has another drastic effect which is often overlooked. Cutting the supply of this commodity allows the remaining kennels to raise their prices far above what would be a normal competitive level were the market allowed to flow. This will increase your pricing structure, as you will see in a later chapter.

A word here about competition. Nowhere in this book will you find specific reference to dealing with competition. This is not because there is none in your area, but because I personally feel that if you concentrate on your business and on giving your best service, you will always prevail. I have been on interviews for pet sitting jobs where I was the third and last person to be considered for the task. I got the job. Why? My service is far and away the best the customer can get. I will show you how to let the customer know you are the best.

In order to succeed, you must apply the principles outlined in this book. If you have problems in any one area, go back and reread that portion of the book. Follow the procedures item by item and you too can share in an income like mine. This book will carry you from the first glimmer of hope through the first six months of your business life. This is a critical time period.

I truly care about your success. I will mention here what I also say at the end of the book. I want to hear from you after your first six months in business. I want to know about your success. I want to help. If you have questions, you can write to me and ask. I will be glad to answer them if I can.

Use this system. Use the experience I have gained from trial and error. Use all your skills and you cannot fail. As a business owner, there is nothing more grand than the feeling of self-worth and self-reliance. You are going to enjoy this challenge. Now, let's get started.

Heathcliff had a food obsession, that was very clear.
Childproof locks on the fridge held his food so dear.
No leftovers, clean counters, always ruled the day.
Heathcliff opted for action, where there's a will....

1   Getting Started

Every form you will need to run your business has been provided in this book. Some of the forms you can use "as is" with the addition of your own letterhead at the top. Some of the forms must be modified to suit your own purpose and specific situation. The forms are located at the end of the chapter in which they are discussed.

Here are the first four things you need to do to begin your own business:

get a business license
publish notification
get business cards printed
buy an answering machine.

Business License

Go to the city hall in your city and inquire as to what department issues city business licenses. Regardless of the city (or cities) you plan to operate within, your license in the United States is always taken out in the city where you reside. In Canada, it is more likely that you will need a license from the city or town where the business is located. This is for tax purposes. The license will cost you approximately $35 (or less) depending upon the city statutes where you live. The form(s) are simple to fill out and can be processed while you wait. All you need to know prior to doing this is what legal name you wish to register your business under.

Picking a name is a matter of personal choice. It can be cute, pointed, or obscure; it matters little because I will show you what to put on your business cards so that your customers will not mistake your business for any other service. I use the name *Paw Partners* for my own sitting business. You can think up catchy or rhyming names of your own. The name is only a formality for the city license.

A warning here, though. Look through the local yellow pages under the heading of "pet shops" to avoid selecting a name in use. You cannot use a name already taken. There is a national franchise called *Pet Tenders*. *Pet Tenders* would not hesitate to take legal action if you copied that name without buying a franchise. The same is true for any name you see under pet shops, vets, groomers, or any other related businesses. All those names are already being used. If, for example, there is a pet shop in your town called *Fins & Feathers,* you cannot use that name. You really wouldn't want to use any name already existing because you are going to create your own good will. You don't want the baggage (good or bad) that goes with anyone else's name. And you don't want your publicity sending customers to another company.

Published Notification

The clerk who gives you your business license in the U.S. will probably tell you that you have to file an alias. If you are not told, inquire as to which newspaper you should use to do this. The city clerk will always know.

Go in person to the newspaper recommended by city hall and ask for the desk that handles "false name filings." The actual publication for this advertisement by the paper is called a "false name statement." The newspaper calls it an "FNS" for short. Every paper knows by law exactly what wording must be contained in the FNS. All you fill out is a form furnished by the paper with the name of your business, the owner(s), the address, the city, state, zip code, and telephone number. The paper will take care of the rest. A filing is done by the paper with the county clerk in the county in which you reside. The newspaper is solely responsible for the wording, not you.

Be prepared for a small shock. The cost of this publication can (and will) cost more money than if you had taken out a regular one-inch by one-inch display ad in the same newspaper! A usual $10 fee goes to the county clerk for filing. The paper collects this amount separately, plus the costs of publishing this notice four times. Your charges will be higher or lower than $50 depending upon the circulation of the newspaper. The higher the circulation, the higher the costs. It's that simple. I cannot be more explicit because it truly depends on the region and the newspaper's prevailing rates. The newspaper, however, will tell you the exact costs at the time of placement.

You will find that the city/state tax laws are going to be in your favor because you are providing a service, not a product. You provide no food, no treats, no grooming supplies, no toys, nothing but your service. Therefore, if you have a state tax in your state, you will not have to worry about charging or collecting it. This is another great break of the pet sitting business. Technically, once you fill out the application for the license and publish the FNS, you are legally in business! For you Canadians, you will have to learn about your new Goods and Services Tax and how it affects your business.

Business Cards

Here is where you can make a great mistake. Even though you may have just dreamed up the cutest, most clever name for your business in the history of the world—don't use it. Use the form shown below. Here's why.

```
┌─────────────────────────────────────────────────────┐
│   Licensed          Member-NAPS           Bonded    │
│                                                     │
│                   PET SITTING                       │
│                 (In The Pet's Home)                 │
│                   (000) 000-0000                    │
│   Owners/Sitters                      Call Anytime  │
│            "YOUR pet deserves the best."            │
└─────────────────────────────────────────────────────┘
```

You need to have instant recognition of what your service involves. You don't want people to think you are in the boarding business, the transportation business, the kennel business, or the grooming business— simply the sitting business. I tried all sorts of clever wording until it dawned on me that nothing is more succinct than the words, "pet sitting in the pets' home." Straightforward, to the point, and not confusing to the reader.

The message is what is important, not the name of your business. It's hard not to use your business name, I know, it was for me, too. You will have plenty of time later, much further on in your business, to imprint your company name upon the customers you serve. Right now you are only interested in getting people to know what you do—not who you are.

Purchasing business cards is a matter of money and taste. If you wish to conserve funds, you want black and white print, simple stock paper, and the cheapest printer who can print 500 cards. This can be found for under $20. On the other hand, if you want four colors, raised lettering, bond stock paper, and distinct lettering, plus a logo, you can easily spend over $100 for 500 cards. The choice is yours.

I highly recommend being very conservative on this first run. You will find parts of the cards you want to change later on. (We changed with each of the first three printings and are still changing two years later!) This is why I recommend only 500 cards, not 1,000. I realize 1,000 is almost the same price as 500, but just print 500. It will take you only two to three weeks to go through those 500 cards anyway and then you can spend more on a finished product when you know exactly what you want. (I went through 3,500 cards in the first four months.) After my first 500 cards were used up, I wanted to add some things including the words "licensed" and "bonded."

Answering Machine

If you already own an answering machine, you can skip this part of the text. You know how the machine works and how to put a message on it. If you don't own a machine, you must buy one. This machine is vital to the words "call anytime" on your cards. You have a twenty-four-hour-a-day servant at your disposal in an answering machine. I am not going to elaborate here on what type of machine to buy except to strongly recommend that you invest enough money to get one with a remote call-in feature. This allows you to call home from any phone and find out who has called. This will be quite handy and timesaving later on when you are too busy to go home to check your messages.

Returning to your business cards for a moment. You will notice that only your name is shown on the card, not the name of your business. If you have other business interests, or your family doesn't want to be tied up with business calls for your firm, you can simply record the message with your name, not the name of your business. I include my three dogs barking in the background as an added reminder to callers that I am a pet owner. You can create your own message however you wish. Mine lasts only twenty seconds and delivers no selling message whatsoever. The whole idea is to get that name and telephone number so that you can call the person back at your leisure when you have the proper form in hand and can list out the information he or she requires.

Let's see how much money is involved in your recent purchases.

business license	$35
business cards	$20
false name statement	$50
answering machine	$50
total expenses thus far:	$155

Now you will need to add costs for the preparation and duplication of your forms. If you have your own typewriter or computer, then the cost of preparing the necessary forms will be minimal. If you need to have them created by another person, then your costs will depend on how much that person charges. The forms will then cost you about $15 in duplication fees (50 copies each), if you do not prepare multiple copies yourself, so let's look at what four forms you will need right away. They are:

fee schedule
tearoff tack-up sheet
flier sheet
biography sheet.

Fee Schedule

The fee schedule should contain every type of pet you are willing to sit for and the appropriate fee for that pet. How do you determine what a fair rate to charge? Here are a few methods:

Call, or visit, your local veterinarian and kennel. Ask the prices for boarding different pets for a day, week, etc.

Call any other pet sitter you can find, in any other city, and ask what rate is being charged by that person.

Determine the average income level of the type of customer you intend to target for your market and ask yourself, "If I had that person's income and that person's home, what would I pay for my services?"

Use your own income requirements to help determine pricing.

Do all the above, take an average, and use that price.

Here's how you use your income target for price setting. If you need (want) to make $40 per hour, then you divide the hour by three (allowing twenty minutes per call), and you arrive at a rate of $13.33 for each call. Assuming that each person wanting your services has more than one pet, $13.33 could be your rate for two. This is just a simple example. Bear in mind that the majority of your bookings will be in homes with more than one pet. A singular pet is the exception, not the rule. An income of over $50,000 per year is based upon a $13 per call average, making twelve calls per day. If you did this for all 365 days of the year, it would equal over $56,000! Realistically, you would want some vacation. If you took a whole month off per year, you would still make over $50,000 at twelve calls per day. Your income will be based upon your charges. The income I suggest here, however, is based upon my own original charges and rates. You will have to tailor your services to fit your own city and neighborhood.

Perhaps you live in an area which requires you to drive so far that you need to add a small mileage charge on top of your regular rates. In any event, you want your services to be slightly below the boarding price for the pets. Why? If your prices are higher than the kennel, why wouldn't the owner just use the kennel? Remember, you are an unknown while starting out in the business. Once your reputation and outstanding service are known throughout the area, and the referrals are flowing in, you can raise your rates accordingly. I raised my rates nine months after beginning my business.

Your most common sitting assignments will be dogs and cats. Remember that the majority of people have pets. A recent survey showed that in the United States over 60 percent of all households have pets. That translates to over 144 million households as potential customers! Many people will want you to come into their homes more than once a day. That means more income in your pocket. My first four customers averaged over $100 each. My fifth customer had twice-a-day service for a dog and cat and received a bill for $220 for ten days of service!

Let's assume that you have checked with local boarding kennels and the current minimum rate is $8 per day for small dogs (toy poodles, etc.), and the maximum rate is $11 per day for large dogs. You could then set your rate at $9 per day and still safely state to potential customers that your rates are lower than the kennel prices. Use an increment of one-half (rounded) of your base rate for each additional pet. If your rate is $9 per day for one dog or cat, then charge an additional $4 for each extra pet. This makes $13 for two pets. I always suggest using uneven numbers because they sound less than $14, $16, $18, etc.

The greatest amount of work on your part is feeding dogs and cats. Tropical fish or saltwater fish take only a pinch of food and should not bear a high price tag for service when included as part of the daily package. If someone had only tropical fish, then you would use your daily minimum rate with no additional charges.

Birds only require a clean change of paper and some fresh food. The rate for birds should be at least half (or less) of your minimum base rate. Hamsters, turtles, rabbits, etc., can be thrown in as "incidentals" and included in your base rate. This gives you more free services to offer as clients rarely have hamsters, turtles, or rabbits as the only pet in the home.

I did not include livestock in this listing, and for a specific reason. We have taken care of horses, but that care only included feeding and water, not brushing, walking, etc. Be careful about any decision to include livestock in your services unless you have a good understanding of the time required to properly service the livestock, and some native ability to do the job properly.

Some people may require you to give pets special meals. Some dogs and cats may only eat specially prepared food or human food. This is because owners pamper them to an extreme. Pick a modest charge for this meal preparation service and offer it as well. Staying overnight is an additional service that allows you to still take care of other customer pets during normally quiet hours. You can stay in a home from dusk to dawn and charge the same rate that an inexpensive motel would charge. The owners may wish the dog or cat (or both) to sleep with you on the bed. That, too, is just another part of your personalized service.

Remember that when it comes to pets, the owners are not primarily concerned with cost. Owners are concerned with the pets' safety, comfort, and well-being during the owner's absence. Cost is secondary to concerned and involved owners. If people cannot afford your service, they will usually tell you so over the telephone.

You need some added enhancements to offer, along with your other services, as "free" inducements for a potential customer to try you first. After all, if you are there at the home feeding the pets, how long could it take to bring in the newspapers and mail, water the houseplants, check the security, and turn some lights on and off? The entire process can be accomplished in twenty minutes (or less) on every single visit. A half-hour, you will see, is the absolute maximum you will need to spend, unless very abnormal conditions apply. One such condition we had was a home with over 100 houseplants! We added a watering charge to our regular fees at the time of the interview.

You can use our fee schedule form just as it is by adding your own letterhead at the top. Or you can make up your own in any format you wish. It is necessary that you print a fee schedule prior to making any calls. The costs should be something you are proud to show, not embarrassed about. Give the sheet out to anyone who asks about costs. You are giving value for dollars. Never explain costs to anyone. Never apologize for your fees to anyone. Never try to justify fees to anyone. Never, ever, cut your prices for anyone!

I have had numerous calls which, in essence, went as follows, "Oh boy. I'm sure you do a great job, but I just can't afford to spend that much money. Is there any way we could work out a deal?" I decline and tell the caller that my fees are set. There is no option. Do you know that more than half of those folks who said they could not afford my fees called back and used my service? Why? Think of the situation like this. Every time someone says, "I can't afford your fees," the person really means, "I think I can get it for less somewhere else." When the caller finds that the kennel is going to charge more—you'll get the business.

The choices for your customers are clear cut. Take your service or leave it. Remember that you are working toward building an exclusive service. It's not an ordinary service to begin with, so don't make it ordinary by cutting the costs. You are not a discount business.

In this same vein, specials, discounts, or package rates are something that you should leave to retail stores. Your service has a standard price, day in and day out, week in and week out. Holidays are the best time of the year for your business, and you should emphasize the fact that you are available during holidays without any extra charges. Most kennels have those days off and are closed. This means that only one person is coming in, once a day, just to feed the animals. This is an added plus for your personalized service.

Tearoff Tack-up Sheet

This form is to place on bulletin boards, blank walls, over counters, or any space where shops will allow you to leave your literature. The idea behind having the telephone numbers at the bottom is to allow for tearoff strips which show the name of your firm (or what you do) and your telephone number. The customer can easily rip off one of the small slips of paper to save for future reference. You can easily type five of these forms on one single page of paper. You then duplicate the pages, cut them up, and staple them together if you wish multiples in one location.

Here, again, it is not the name of your firm, but what your firm does, that is important. You want to convey to the customer the ultimate reason for telephoning your number, not how cute the name of your firm is. Stress that there is no obligation for making the call. No obligation for having a free consultation about the customer's pets. This is important because it will build trust. You want to visit in person, without the prospect feeling obligated to a specific commitment. Believe me, the prospect will turn into a customer once your interview is concluded.

Flier Sheet

The purpose of this sheet is to show the areas you serve and the types of pets you sit. It touts your free services as well as some other basic reasons the customer should utilize your business. The sheet is designed primarily for travel agents, veterinarians, and pet shops, but it can be used with many other firms as well. With only minor modifications, you can rewrite our form, or you can design one which more specifically suits your needs. The choice is yours to make.

Biography Sheet

This is a very useful tool as a summary sheet to give out to prospective customers and business owners. It illustrates and highlights the following facts:

Why the person should use your service.
How the pet will feel using your service.
Why you went into the business.

What areas you work in.
A *conclusion of facts* about your service.

With minor modifications, you can rewrite our form using your name, or you can tailor make one to fit your own needs and situation. With any literature that you may design, remember the newspaper motto. A good newspaper always tells you who, what, where, when, and why.

Tearoff Tack-up Sheet

| John Doe, Sitter | PET SITTERS
In Your Home
(000) 000-0000 | Jane Doe, Sitter |

All Types Of Pets
day - week - month
Free Consultation Without Obligation

Your pet deserves the best.

Pet Sitters (000) 000-0000 | Pet Sitters (000) 000-0000 | Pet Sitters (000) 000-0000 | Pet Sitters (000) 000-0000 | Pet Sitters (000) 000-0000 | Pet Sitters (000) 000-0000 | Pet Sitters (000) 000-0000 | Pet Sitters (000) 000-0000 | Pet Sitters (000) 000-0000 | Pet Sitters (000) 000-0000

Fee Schedule

All prices are based on a *minimum* of twenty minutes per day of loving play:

PET	PER DAY
One dog or cat	$ 9.00
Two dogs or cats	13.00
Three dogs or cats	17.00
Maximum per household	20.00
Tropical or saltwater fish	1.00*
Birds	3.00*
Hamsters	Included*
Turtles	Included*

(*If these animals are the only pets in the household, then the cost is $9.00 each visit.)

SUPPLEMENTAL NEEDS

Extra visits per day	$ 9.00 Each Visit
Overnight stays	29.00 per night
(Includes special meal preparation)	
Special meals cooked	2.00 per day

Please note that the following are included *free* with our service:

- Bringing in newspapers
- Watering houseplants
- Checking pets coats
- Telephone answering
- Bringing in the mail
- Checking house security
- Administering medication
- Turning lights on and off

———————— *Your pet deserves the best.* ————————

Pet Sitters

Your vacation can be much more pleasant and relaxed knowing your pets are comfortable, safe, fed, and secure in the atmosphere your pets know best—your own home.

We specialize in only one thing, taking good care of your pets by visiting and playing with them once or more each day while you are away.

My wife and I started this business because we wanted to give the kind of care that couldn't be found when boarding our own pets. Now, a limited number of customers can share in this peace of mind. Call today for a personal interview, with your pets, to discuss our services. There is no obligation, of course.

The following are always included *free* with our service:

- Bringing in newspapers
- Watering houseplants
- Checking pets' coats
- Telephone answering
- Bringing in the mail
- Checking house security
- Administering medication
- Turning lights on and off

AREAS SERVED:

Lomita
Palos Verdes
Palos Verdes Estates
Rancho Palos Verdes
Rolling Hills
Rolling Hills Estates
San Pedro
South Torrance

TYPES OF PETS:

Dogs
Cats
Birds (all types)
Tropical fish
Saltwater fish
Hamsters
Turtles
Bunnies

————————*Your pet deserves the best.* ————————

Something you should know . . .

Your pet is much more comfortable, serene, and happy in the comfort of your home. Boarded in the unfamiliar and lonely atmosphere of a foreign place for a day, week, or month can be a terrifying experience for your pet.

Your pet will enjoy staying home during your travels knowing that someone who loves animals is going to come over to play each day. We'll bring in the papers, the mail, water the plants, check the lights, and make certain your pet is happy, fed, and secure each day you are gone.

My wife and I have been involved with all types of pets for over thirty years. We have had birds, tropical and saltwater fish, cats, and dogs. Currently, we have three poodles and a cat. We know from years of experience that pets respond best to love and affection. Nothing has ever replaced petting!

We began this business because we were unhappy bringing our pets home from boarding with ear and eye infections, kennel cough, and fleas. We wanted personalized care that could allow us peace of mind while we traveled. We now offer this kind of service to you. Service that we would like to have.

We service only a limited area of six cities: Lomita, Palos Verdes, Palos Verdes Estates, Rancho Palos Verdes, Rolling Hills, Rolling Hills Estates, San Pedro, and South Torrance. We remain in only a very confined area because there are just the two of us and we want to have enough time to service your needs properly.

We offer you guaranteed reliability and tailored, personalized service. A written report on the activities of your pets is also part of our service.

Please tell your friends about our service. If for *any* reason you have some questions, please ask — we care!

Cordially,

Bill & Ellen Foster,
Owner/Sitters

———————————— *Your pet deserves the best.* ————————————

*Be there a dog in the world, so docile and down on his luck,
That he won't pick up his ears and bark, after the garbage truck?*

2 Your First Calls

Armed with the master copy of your four forms, go to a local copier shop and have them duplicated. Usually a copier can be found which charges five cents per copy. You need clear, clean copies. You don't want to sacrifice clarity for price. Even if you are forced to pay ten cents per copy, it is well worth it. You want fifty copies of each form. You may need more copies later, but fifty is ample to begin your new career. Your costs then will range from $10 to $20 for the duplication of these forms.

If you have picked up your business cards and you have the forms copied, you are ready to begin your business life.

Look at a map of your local area. Take a compass and study the map. How far do you wish to drive in a day? Are you going to cover ten miles? Twenty miles? Fifty miles? In my own case, sixteen miles was about the limit of my willingness to travel. Living in Los Angeles, I have the advantage of having many little cities comprising one total area. This means I can easily service eight small cities without traveling more than sixteen miles from home in any one direction.

Take a highlighting pen and enclose a rough circle around the area you are going to serve. You don't go beyond the limits of that area no matter how tempting the inducement. If you go outside your chosen range, you will find that gas, travel, and time will eat up all your profit. I have received many calls from desperate pet owners who lived twenty or thirty miles from my home who would probably have paid double if I would have come to the rescue. I always resisted the temptation. This is your target market area. Keep this map on the wall by your telephone. I constantly look at the map during each new inquiry to make certain the caller is in my area of service.

Yellow Pages

Go through the yellow pages which serve those areas you are going to work in. You are looking, initially, under three categories only—pet shops, veterinarians, and grooming. Using three-by-five-inch lined cards, write or type on them the name, address, city, and telephone number of each. Use one card for each business listed. Let's say you find seven pet shops, eight veterinarians, and twelve grooming shops. You now have twenty-seven calls to make in person. This is where it becomes important to sell yourself. You are going to visit these twenty-seven places to introduce yourself, to talk about your service, and to leave your literature with the business owners.

At this early stage in your business life, you have no source of referrals to bring business to you. You don't have a yellow page listing, you have no newspaper advertising, you have no previous customers to send new business your way. You need an easy and fast method of getting some business.

The best source of business is from people who see pets every single day. Pet shop owners, veterinarians, and groomers! These business owners are going to become salespeople for your business. After your initial calls upon these business owners, you are going to make a routine of dropping in on those who give you referrals to become better acquainted. From my very first call upon these business people, to this very day, my absolute best source of customer referrals has been pet shops, veterinarians, and grooming shops.

Use the three-by-five-inch cards as a tickler file for your calls. You route your in-person calls in the best driving order to eliminate wasted time. If you have a map of your area, use it to put the coordinates in the upper right hand corner of each card, then you know which call should come first. The first call is to the one nearest your own home. Work in an outward circle. In my case, I had to make over fifty calls in the beginning. Out of these fifty calls, some were out of business. Some firms had moved out of my geographic area. When all calls were completed, I had called, in person, on a total of forty-two business owners. Making these calls, these personal visits, should take from one to four days, depending on your routing and how long your conversation with each business owner lasts.

The New Day

Let's assume it's early on a Monday morning. You are ready to begin selling yourself and your new service. The first thing to remember is to turn on your answering machine with your message in place. After all, the first call you make may give you a referral and you want to get that telephone message. You are now ready to go out the door, but wait—how are you dressed?

In my past business dealings, I always wore a suit in such situations because I naturally assumed that a suit was the proper business attire. My wife pointed out that if I wore a custom-made suit, I would not appear to be a person who would be happy to sit with pets. Too formal, too dignified, too removed from casual life.

You want to dress casually, but not sloppily. You want clothes neat and clean, well-pressed, but casual enough so that you look like the kind of person who would be natural around pets. A casual but sporty attire is the best way to describe it. I traded my tie and suit jacket for a turtleneck sweater, slacks, and a captain's jacket. Believe me, my wife was right! I looked like a person who would sit with pets. I now call this turtleneck and slacks outfit my uniform. I wear the same type of outfit on every single sales call and interview and it works perfectly.

Now you drive to your first store and walk in armed with at least three copies of each of your four forms. You can have them in something simple like a paper file folder or an inexpensive fold-over portfolio. I use a portfolio which opens to hold the papers under a sleeve and has room for a scratch pad on the other side. You introduce yourself by name (hand over your card). Tell the clerk or owner that you are in the pet sitting business and that you may well have a service that the store's customers can use. You explain that you are new in the business and would appreciate any referrals that the store may be able to send you. You immediately offer the fee schedule, the flier sheet, and your biography sheet to that person to keep on file. You ask if the store has a bulletin board and if you can tack up your tear-off phone number sheet. Remember to bring your own thumbtacks. You don't want to be a bother and burden to the store—come prepared!

Let's discuss for a moment what you expect for your effort and why you are calling upon these three types of businesses.

Pet Shops

As a general rule, pet shops do not board pets. This means that a customer may ask the shop owner or clerk if he or she knows of anyone who boards or even sits for pets. You have just provided that business owner with useful knowledge; he or she is now informed and can advise customers of your services. It costs the pet shop owner nothing and adds expertise to his or her customer service.

Most pet shops will welcome your call; that is, unless that particular shop offers boarding. The way around that situation is to say the following: "I realize that many people like to board pets. I think it is a good idea myself. However, my service is strictly for those people who either have too many pets to board or prefer the pets to remain at home. I don't believe I am in competition with you. I would only like to have you recommend my service to those people who do not wish to board their pets."

This sentence will usually alleviate any fears that the pet shop owner may have about you attempting to take over existing customers. It is a true statement. People who like to board pets will not use your service. Only people who want the pets to remain at home will call you. You are not competing with boarding!

Veterinarians

Many veterinarians have some form of boarding facility, if only for sick animals. Here again, use the same reasoning to convince vets to recommend your services. Amazingly, the majority of my present referrals are from veterinarians! Ask to leave your forms and use the bulletin board if the vet has one.

Grooming Shops

Groomers see dogs and cats all day long. Here is an untapped gold mine! Who better for a customer to mention pet needs to than a groomer? Grooming shops board nothing, all the grooming cages are simply holding pens for upcoming grooming. A grooming shop will employ from one to ten people. In most cases, the larger the shop—the greater the referrals—it is just a matter of large customer volume.

I don't want to leave this subject with you thinking that every single place you walk into is going to welcome you with open arms. That is just not the case. In my particular case, many businesses had been bombarded with people visiting them asking them to recommend everything from flea shampoos to vitamins. Most of the business owners in my local area were very skeptical of my new business. In fact, my reception was lukewarm, at best. Most had this response: "We don't recommend anybody for anything!" In those cases, I just asked that they set out my cards and let the customer call me, get a free interview, and judge for themselves whether my service was worthwhile. I asked for no recommendations until I could prove myself worthy by having happy customers return to the business and thank them for my service. This only took one month. I now have thirty-eight businesses which highly recommend my service.

Don't get discouraged if one business owner says he won't accept your cards; just go on to the next call. My success lies in the referrals I get from pet shops, veterinarians, and groomers. The biggest potential for failure in any service business is to just put an ad in the yellow pages and sit and wait by the phone. You can wait until you are bankrupt!

Summary

The entire point of making these "in person" calls is to allow the prospective "messenger" to meet you, see you, feel personally involved, and to be confident in recommending your service. A customer who has been referred by a vet, pet shop operator, or groomer whom the customer trusts, is almost always a guaranteed booking. I now receive numerous calls which begin, "My veterinarian recommended that I call you. I need your services."

With that recommendation behind me, I know that I am going to get the job.

It is an excellent idea to follow up within a month or two on some of these calls, and bring any active participants in your success some doughnuts. After you track each lead you will know who has been helpful in sending you business. After my first four weeks in business, I found that six veterinarians were responsible for over fifteen customer inquiries and $2,000 in potential business. I wanted to thank them and keep those inquiries coming. I purchased six half-dozen boxes of mixed doughnuts and delivered each box personally as a "thank you" for the referrals. I put more business cards on top of each box as a gentle reminder to keep passing out my cards. The vets were thrilled to get the doughnuts. Not that many people bring presents to veterinarians.

I used veterinarians as an example along with doughnuts. You should reward any source of referrals and your reward could be fresh fruit, candy, soft drinks, or any low cost item you think would be appreciated by the recipient. You can make this visit for reward a monthly routine, or an every-other-month task to keep your name in the center of their memory.

Once you have made calls on every business on your cards, it is time to go home and begin the somewhat mundane, but necessary job of paperwork.

Paperwork

Take your pile of three-by-five-inch cards and begin writing on each one the date you visited the firm. This is a visual reminder to you of when you first contacted them and when you may wish to do a follow-up. Alphabetize this list of calls and put the list in typewritten or longhand form. A sample is shown at the end of this chapter called *Personal Calls & Results.* You want to remember who you called on and how many referrals you received from each. Further, you may wish to send each of them a Christmas card. I picked out a cute card the first year which had a dog and a cat on the front. I stapled my business card to the inside and signed each one personally. This keeps your name in front of each business and reminds that business, once again, of your service.

I had only been out two days making calls when my first customer called me—a referral! The first sitting job was with three dogs and a bird for eight days. This hit my maximum rate of $20 per day. The second day I had, in effect, made $160! By the first Friday of the second week (five days into my new career), I had received five telephone calls resulting in three sitting jobs. All this without investing a nickel in advertising! I was now guaranteed of making over $300, all from just the first week of inquiries!

As a backup to your good effort in making calls, you may wish to augment your own personal calls with some form of advertising. I recommend a small paper that is read by an area-select clientele. If you are only servicing twenty square miles in a city of a million people, you waste time, money, and effort advertising in a newspaper that covers those million people. You want a small, local paper which is distributed in a highly select area. This is easily found out by asking any of those pet shops, veterinarians, or grooming shops which newspaper they advertise in. If two or more people say they had good results from a certain paper, then you are safe in using that paper too.

Choosing which part of a small circulation newspaper to advertise in depends totally on your business location. Your small ad might be more effective under the "pets" column than in the "services" column. Ask the newspaper which section it recommends. After all, the newspaper wants you to get calls, too. They want you to become a regular advertiser with them. If you decide to use a newspaper ad, I stress again to use the words "pet sitting in the pet's home." Stress what you do, not who you are. Remember to list "call anytime" because your recorder can handle the calls twenty-four hours a day.

It is always important to ask every inquiring prospect where that person heard about your service. In this way you can monitor what value (if any) certain advertising may have for you now, and in the future. Two example ads are shown here:

Animal Care

```
┌─────────────────────────┐
│      PET SITTER         │
│     In Your Home        │
│  Licensed•References    │
│   Free Consultation     │
│      Bill Foster        │
│    Owner•Sitter         │
│     Call Anytime        │
└─────────────────────────┘
```

```
┌─────────────────────────────────┐
│         PET SITTER              │
│       IN YOUR HOME              │
│     Licensed - References       │
│ Free Consultation - Gift Certificates │
│        BILL FOSTER              │
│       Owner - Sitter            │
└─────────────────────────────────┘
```

Personal Calls & Results

STORE NAME	CITY	REFERRALS
Airport Plaza Grooming	Torrance	0
All Pets Veterinary Hospital	Rancho Palos Verdes	2
Animal & Bird Clinic	San Pedro	1
Apollo Grooming	Rancho Palos Verdes	0
Ask Mr. Groomer	San Pedro	4
Audro Pet Shop	Rancho Palos Verdes	1
The B & H Grooming Shop	San Pedro	0
Bon Voyage Pet Shop	Rolling Hills Estates	3
Center Animal Hopsital	Rolling Hills Estates	1
Channel Animal Hospital	San Pedro	2
Critterville Pet Shop	San Pedro	0
Cruises Groomers	Torrance	1
Fossee Pet Floss	Rolling Hills Estates	3
Gaffey Pet Shop	San Pedro	0
Golden Cove General Store	Rancho Palos Verdes	2
Harbor Groomers	Rolling Hills Estates	6
Kritter Korral Pet Shops	Harbor City	1
Le Tour De Dog	San Pedro	5
Logan Brush and Curl	San Pedro	0
The Magical Fish Company	Rancho Palos Verdes	2

Six containers of water passed by on a stroll, Pansey and Petunia use only the toilet bowl!

3 More Forms You Need

You have made your local, in-person business calls upon the pet shops, veterinarians, and groomers. You have, in exchange for these calls, received some telephone inquiries and you are ready to begin your business in earnest. You want to do something right now which will benefit you immensely for the first month you are in business. Take an 8½-by-11 inch standard sized sheet of paper and a felt marking pen and write at the top *Ask this First*. Then write under that heading these three questions:

What area do you live in?
What dates are you going to be gone?
How did you hear about our service?

Tape this sheet of paper on the wall over the telephone you plan to use for your business. At first I spent many minutes in lengthy discussions with prospective customers only to find that the prospect lived about fifty miles from my home. If the prospect is out of your area, there is nothing more to discuss. You want to ask what dates the customer is going to be gone because you may not have time during those days. What if the sitting starts tomorrow and tomorrow is totally booked for you? You want to ask how the prospect heard about your service because you may forget at any other time to get this information. These three questions can save a lot of time and energy. If you have a problem with the first two questions, it is going to be a short conversation.

You still need another seven forms. Some of those seven forms will be necessary to take along with you on your first interview. The forms you need are:

Monthly Calendar
Tips for a Happier Vacation
References
Background History Sheet
Pet Personality Profile
Inquiries
Peace of Mind.

We will now discuss each one of these in detail. An example of each form that you can copy, modify, or rewrite entirely is at the end of this chapter.

Monthly Calendar

You need some form of calendar which allows enough space to write in your appointments and sitting schedule for each day of the month. It is kept in your office at home and allows you to see, at a glance, if you can book another appointment for any given day. It could (and should) also be duplicated in a hand-held version that you can take along with you on appointments. Bear in mind that twelve bookings per day (allowing for driving) may be your maximum potential. You don't want to overbook yourself or find yourself with sitting jobs at the extreme ends of your territory at the end of the day.

Tips for a Happier Vacation

This is a sheet which has ten items on it that clients may forget to think about when preparing to depart on vacation. You can use the examples on the sample form, or make up your own based on your actual experiences. You may find that you need to update and add to this reminder list as your own experience dictates. You will see this form in use again during the interview.

References

When you visit a potential customer for the first time, it is very likely that the customer will ask you for references from other sitting jobs. You have none! What do you say now? Here is what I said in the beginning of my career, and it works perfectly.

> "Mrs. Jones, I am relatively new in this business and any sitting references would be very short-term. I would prefer to give you a list of my personal character references. These are people who have known me over a long period of time and can vouch for my honesty and integrity. Along with these references is a bank reference

where I have banked for the past years. Feel free to call any, or all of them, if you like."

You then hand the customer the sheet. You will find that most people are very trusting. Few people call your references. However, since you are encouraging them to call, it is important that you get the permission of the people you intend to use as references. You need a good recommendation of your honesty and integrity from these references. Once your first two months of sitting are under your belt you can then begin to use past customers as references and you won't need these other references. Therefore, you can tell your friends and relatives that you only need to use them as a reference for a maximum of two months. That is not too long a time to impose on their good will.

The reference sheet is not important for the business calls made at the pet shops, veterinarians, or grooming shops. The most you will get asked by these people is if you are licensed and bonded. You are licensed. Let's talk a bit about bonding.

Bonding is something you may wish to consider in the future just as a gimmick for sales. I use the word gimmick freely because the bond will cost you $100 to $150 per year and only has a face value of $2,500. The bond is not going to do the customer any good. At least not according to what the customer perceives the word bond to mean. Most bonding companies pay off only after arrest and conviction of the perpetrator. If this is you, it means that your own bonding company is going to come after you for recovery! If you know you are honest and are not going to steal anything, why pay someone to prosecute you if you didn't do anything wrong? The $100 to $150 per year fee may be worth considering later, just to put on your business cards if you think it will impress some people. Unless a local statute in your particular area makes it mandatory that you be bonded, a bond is not a good investment for you or your customers.

Now, after saying all that, let me completely confuse you and reverse my position on bonding. My business is bonded. I am bonded. Why? Simply because of the area in which I live and work. Many of my customers have million-dollar homes. This affluent area thinks of the words "licensed" and "bonded" as something akin to salt and pepper. I tried to explain to more than half a dozen customers exactly what I have just told you and all it did was raise doubts in their minds. Not one customer ever asked the amount of my bond. My bond is only for $2,500. That sum wouldn't pay for much in the home of a wealthy person. It is worthless for any practical purpose. I just got tired of explaining what I have just explained, gave in, and purchased a bond.

Oddly enough, since that time very few people have ever asked me about bonding during the initial telephone inquiry. You must decide for yourself if bonding is something that is an accepted practice in your area, or if people are generally more trusting. Let your customers be your guide. The best form of bond you can develop is the trust of past customers and the reliance on you for your services, over and over again. Customers' trust and good will is the best bond and you cannot buy that.

You'll need that references sheet on your first interview, so develop it early. When asked for references, scribbling names on a scrap of paper is a sure way to raise anxiety in your customer. It may even lose you a booking. Be prepared. Be professional.

Background History Sheet

For every prospect, it will be necessary to do a personal interview in that prospect's home. You need a lot of detailed information about the pets, the home, and the prospect to complete your records before you can begin your service. More details on the background history sheet will be discussed in the interview chapter. Remember you need a completed form for every customer. A good number for first duplication is twenty.

Pet Personality Profile

This form is married to the background history sheet. You will use one or more copies per customer, dependent totally upon the number of pets in the home. Each sheet has room for four pets. You should duplicate thirty copies of this sheet to be assured of having enough for your first twenty calls. One of my first customers had seven pets so I needed two sheets. I will explain this sheet in detail during the interview chapter so further discussion here is redundant.

Inquiries

You will receive many calls from potential customers who are curious about your rates, service, etc. You need to keep a record of those who have telephoned and of all the information you gain through the telephone conversation. You want to be able to look intelligent when the prospect calls back in three months and reminds you that she is the one who called about the two Persian cats. This is where the answering machine comes in handy. You can hear the calls come in, look up the information in the file, and call them back when you are prepared and professional.

I would recommend keeping completed inquiry sheets handy for a period of only three months; then file them to the back of your file. Keep these records for at least one year. You can then safely throw inquiries out if nothing has materialized in that length of time.

Peace of Mind

This form is a basic statement of the things you are promising to do for the pets while the owners are absent. It is given out to customers during the interview portion of your job. It lists the program you go through each time you visit the home. I highly recommend this form. It is extremely effective as a closing tool during an interview. You want to leave a copy of this form each time you visit a new home. I would also recommend making twenty copies of this form initially.

Tips for a Happier Vacation

1. Please tell the neighbors and gardener that we are going to be coming each day to take care of your pets. We drive a (make of car here), license number:_____. Please tell gate security also, if applicable.

2. Leave a radio playing on a mild station with soft music. Your pet will enjoy the music and it has a soothing effect. If your pet watches television, putting the television on a timer is helpful.

3. Leave a light on in the house. A stove light in the kitchen is a good choice. If you wish, we can vary the lighting each evening, so it will appear that someone is always home.

4. Please put out an extra water bowl so your pet never runs out of water. We will keep them both full.

5. If you are going to be gone for more than two days, don't forget to unplug the electric coffee pot, it can steam itself dry.

6. Leave a phone number and name by the telephone of someone to call in the unlikely event of an emergency.

7. Please set out any special medication your pet may need along with instructions for administration.

8. Make certain the things your pets get into (that you don't like) are either shut, or put up, out of the way. Some good examples are wastepaper baskets, dirty clothes hampers, etc.

9. Make certain all doors and windows are locked and the security is on.

10. Shut the doors to any rooms that you don't want your pets to enter. We will make certain they stay shut.

Have A Great Trip!

―――――――――*Your pet deserves the best.*―――――――――

Paw Partners
2361 East 34th Avenue
Denver, Colorado 99917
(416) 555-1212

References

Please feel free to call any or all of the following:

PERSONAL CHARACTER

Mr. Jim Streeter   (213) 555-1212
Comptroller
Rancho Cucamonga, California

Mrs. Laura Davies   (805) 555-1212
Housewife
Canyon Country, California

Miss Tammi Barnett   (818) 555-1212
Assistant Controller
Pasadena, California

Mrs. Karen Blackwood   (213) 555-1212
Customer Service Representative
West Covina, California

BANK REFERENCE

First National Charter and Reserve   (213) 555-1212
West Wood Songbird Office #0021
2776 East 57th Street
Los Angeles, California 90021

———————— *Your pet deserves the best.* ————————

Background History Sheet

Interview Date: _____ Time: _____ A.M./P.M. Map Book: _____
Owner's Names: _____ Home Phone: _____
Address: _____ Work Phone: _____
City: _____ Postal/Zip Code: _____ Directions: _____

Family Vet Clinic: _____ Doctor: _____
Emergency Telephone Neighbor/Friend/Relative: _____
Emergency Telephone for Owners (if applicable): _____

Yard Fenced?	__Yes __No	Sprinkler System? __Yes __No
Pet Door?	__Yes __No	Newspapers? __Yes __No
Brushing?	__Yes __No	Mail? __Yes __No
Walks?	__Yes __No	Sign For Pkgs? __Yes __No
Food Supply Adequate?	__Yes __No	Change Lighting? __Yes __No
Pet(s) On Medication Now?	__Yes __No	Answer Phone? __Yes __No
Inside Plants To Water?	__Yes __No	Security System? __Yes __No

Watering Can?: _____ Code: _____
Garbage Can Location: _____

Trash Day: _____ First Time Alone?: __Yes __No
How do pets react to your absence?: _____
Anybody on or in property during your absence? (i.e. gardener, pool man, housekeeper, cleaning, construction, etc.): _____

Date of Last Vet Visit: _____ Vet Form? __Yes __No
Preferred Visit Time: A.M. _____ P.M. _ Both _____ only _____
Date/Day Start: _____ Date/Day End: _____ Key Pickup: ___
Referred By: _____ Key Coding Now: _____

Date: _____ Owner: _____

Pet's Personality Profile

Pet Type: _____ Name: _____ Sex: ___ Color: _____
Breed: _____ Birthday: ___ Fed: ____ A.M. ____ P.M.
____ Wet ____ Dry   amount: _____ inside/outside/both (circle)
Any Special Toys: ___ Yes ___ No   What?: _____
Any Special Treats: ___ Yes ___ No   What?: _____
Separate Feedings?:   ___ Yes ___ No   Where?: _____

Pet Type: _____ Name: _____ Sex: ___ Color: _____
Breed: _____ Birthday: ___ Fed: ____ A.M. ____ P.M.
____ Wet ____ Dry   amount: _____ inside/outside/both (circle)
Any Special Toys: ___ Yes ___ No   What?: _____
Any Special Treats: ___ Yes ___ No   What?: _____
Separate Feedings?:   ___ Yes ___ No   Where?: _____

Pet Type: _____ Name: _____ Sex: ___ Color: _____
Breed: _____ Birthday: ___ Fed: ____ A.M. ____ P.M.
____ Wet ____ Dry   amount: _____ inside/outside/both (circle)
Any Special Toys: ___ Yes ___ No   What?: _____
Any Special Treats: ___ Yes ___ No   What?: _____
Separate Feedings?:   ___ Yes ___ No   Where?: _____

Pet Type: _____ Name: _____ Sex: ___ Color: _____
Breed: _____ Birthday: ___ Fed: ____ A.M. ____ P.M.
____ Wet ____ Dry   amount: _____ inside/outside/both (circle)
Any Special Toys: ___ Yes ___ No   What?: _____
Any Special Treats: ___ Yes ___ No   What?: _____
Separate Feedings?:   ___ Yes ___ No   Where?: _____

Pet Type: _____ Name: _____ Sex: ___ Color: _____
Breed: _____ Birthday: ___ Fed: ____ A.M. ____ P.M.
____ Wet ____ Dry   amount: _____ inside/outside/both (circle)
Any Special Toys: ___ Yes ___ No   What?: _____
Any Special Treats: ___ Yes ___ No   What?: _____
Separate Feedings?:   ___ Yes ___ No   Where?: _____

Inquiries

NAME	DATE	QUESTIONS
Mrs. Stattler 4674 Ranch Place Drive Santa Domingo, CA 90274	11/15/	Wanted rates and all info. mailed out to her. Did so on 11/16. I suspect she has three pets.
Mr. Jones 1521 Gravel Lake Place Santa Marta, CA 90223	11/16/	Wanted to know if we handled hamsters and was there a limit to # of pets? Has need in about 4 weeks.
Cheri Stanton ?	11/16/	Will call back in two weeks. Wanted to know if young dog was OK. Has a 9½ week old lab.
Jim Davis (213) 555-1212	11/17/	Wants me to call back if we decide we can service his home in Santa Clara. I told him I would call by 11/24/.
David Robbins 24 Imperial Circle La Harper, CA 90221	11/18/	Wanted to get mail on charges for four pets for one month. In mail to him 11/18/.

Peace of Mind

You have probably never given much thought to just how much time and effort you put into your pet's good health and happiness. We have. When you are gone, many things have to be done on a daily basis to make certain your pets are safe, secure, comfortable, and happy. We go through a twenty-two (22) point checklist *every time* we visit with your pets. This list includes:

- Releasing your security system.
- Bringing in the newspapers.
- Bringing in the mail.
- Giving each pet clean, fresh, water.
- Giving each pet the proper amount of food.
- Making sure each pet eats all the food.
- Re-storing the supplies in the proper place.
- Giving treats (if they are allowed).
- Cleaning up any "accidents" that may occur.
- Watering all the plants.
- Having meaningful "playtime" with each pet.
- Taking pets for walks.
- Forwarding messages if requested.
- Checking all internal doors and windows.
- Checking all external doors and windows.
- Changing the lighting arrangement (on and off).
- Making certain pets are in the proper places.
- Making notes for owners.
- Administering medication if needed.
- Inspecting each pet's coat.
- Re-locking the house (or area).
- Restoring the security system.

You do most of these things automatically when you are home. Isn't it comforting to know that someone is going to go through a check list each day and do them for you while you're away?

─────────── *Your pet deserves the best.* ───────────

*Canned or dry dog meals? Simply too rude.
Maxine dined only on 'people food'!*

4 Telephone Inquiries

Every telephone call you receive does not result in an interview or a booking. It would be nice if it were that clear and simple, but it isn't. Some telephone inquiries only want to know your price. You will discover that most telephone inquiries that begin with the question "How much does this cost?" usually end in disappointment for both you and the caller. Many people are just curious about your type of service and perhaps want to save the information for future reference. Each telephone call is important to you, though, because it could result in a future booking, if treated properly.

There will come a moment during every telephone inquiry where you discover if the caller is ready for an interview. If the caller has not made specific plans, or the potential sitting is a month or more in the future, this is a good opportunity to send that caller more information. Most people who called my business during the first few months of operation were very surprised to learn that I would mail them free information and literature. They were pleased and readily accepted the offer.

If the conversation on the telephone is very specific and very detailed in nature, then you cannot use a standard form letter to reply. If, for example, the caller wants to know what days in June you have free, the cost for one dog, two cats, and a turtle, how much overnight service for two nights costs, etc., then you must take the time to respond in a personalized letter.

If, however, the caller only has a general inquiry, you can use the standard reply letter shown at the end of this chapter. This standard reply letter will save you a lot of time because you will get two or three calls a day that are just inquiries for future reference. Whatever the type of letter you use, sign each one personally. Even a form letter is enhanced by a current date and a real signature.

I suggest putting a copy of each letter into a folder marked "inquiries only," for future reference. Sometime in the months to come, that person is going to call back and mention the earlier telephone call. Another reason for keeping copies of the inquiries is to be able to put those people on your mailing list so you can inform them of any changes in your business such as price increases.

When you mail any caller the standard reply letter, be certain to enclose your fee schedule, peace of mind sheet, and a business card. I get many telephone inquiries from callers who do not have my business card for reference because they were directed to my service by word of mouth.

My conversion rate from telephone inquiry to customer is one out of every five. I have never followed up by telephoning the recipient back and attempting to close the sale. I would suppose my conversion rate would be much higher if I did call back; I just never had the time.

Another reason for saving all inquiries is money. Yes, names represent money. Right now there is not a thought in your mind that the day will ever come when you would want to sell your business. If that day does come, the more names you have in your customer and prospect files, the more money your business is going to be worth in sales dollars. Many firms today are offering franchises for sale which have no customers or prospects. The buyer has to start from scratch! If the day ever comes when you decide to sell your business, a customer list with five hundred names and a prospect list with eight hundred names is worth a lot of money. A good rule to remember is to never throw away the name of a potential customer.

Standard Reply Letter

Thank you very much for calling the other day to inquire about our pet sitting services. Enclosed is a fee schedule along with a twenty-two item check list of duties we will perform on every visit with your pets.

We began this business because we could not find a viable alternative to boarding our pets in a kennel. We felt that having our pets at home, safe, secure, and comfortable, was more important to us than lugging them down to an unfamiliar and frightening surrounding and getting our babies back a day or two after we returned home. We wanted our pets to enjoy our vacation too!

Our business is licensed, bonded, and recommended by all our past customers, as well as pet shops, groomers, kennels, and many veterinarians. We will be happy to furnish you with a list of those references. We have an extremely limited clientele due to many repeat customers and many who need twice-a-day service.

We would be happy to have an interview in your home at your convenience, to meet with your pets and explain our services in detail. There is no obligation for this initial meeting. If you would like further information, or a personal interview, please give us a call anytime.

Your pet sitters,

Owners/Sitters

Encls.

―――――― *Your pet deserves the best.* ――――――

*Gorky loved tennis balls, all in his face.
But really... isn't three, a bit of a disgrace?*

5 Veterinarian Release Form

I avidly believe that the customer should not have to sign anything to transact business with you. After all, the customer doesn't sign a form to deal with the pool man, the gardener, the housekeeper, or the chauffeur. Why should the customer have to sign a form just to have you take care of a pet? But there is an exception to most every rule and here's this one.

What do you do when you are sitting with a couple of four-month-old golden retrievers and you find that they have ripped the primary power cable off the rear of the house, bitten through the cord right down to bare copper, and almost electrocuted themselves? What if one dog was burned and had to go to the veterinarian for the emergency? What if the bill was $600 and the customer refused to pay? After all, *you* elected to take that dog to the vet on the basis of your own judgment didn't you?

This is a very unlikely scenario but it can happen. After checking with numerous veterinarians, I found that the simplest and most convenient method of dealing with any emergency was to have a signed form on hand, which was acceptable to veterinarians for both boarding the pet during recuperation and arranging for payment of the bill.

You can use the form at the end of this chapter to adopt as your own or you can create one by yourself. The key here is to make the customer as comfortable as possible, so keep the wording simple. Don't make the form look too legal, too lengthy, or too wordy. Make it simple to understand and agree with.

This form can be tested by taking it to your local veterinarians and asking them if they would agree to treat any pet with the submission of this signed form. If they agree, you are all set; the form is correct.

Now, what do you do about a pet that gets injured when most vets are not open? It's eight at night and you are just finishing up your last call. You find one of your customer's dogs is severely injured. What now?

For this contingency, I went to my own veterinarian and asked, straight out, if he would be willing to be "on call" if I needed him in an emergency. It just so happens that he is a very conscientious doctor who keeps in touch with his answering service twenty-four hours a day. He agreed to treat any animals I might have problems with, and further agreed to make house calls, if necessary. I suggest that you find such a vet and keep that person in reserve in case of an unexpected emergency, like the power cord. You never know what can happen and it is always best to be prepared.

The alternative to this method is to have your customers tell their own vets that you have authorization to bring in their pets. The obvious drawback is you don't know if the customers remembered to tell the vets. Unless you call each customer before the sitting, you really don't know for certain. It is much easier to just keep this form in the customer's file and be safe.

Veterinarian Release Form

TO: _____ (name of veterinarian clinic)

In the event of illness or injury related to my pet(s), I hereby authorize __(fill in your name here)__ of __(name of firm here)__, as my pet sitters, to bring in my pet(s) for whatever medical treatment may be required.

I will assume full responsibility upon my return for payment of all services rendered. If my specific veterinarian (named above) is not available for any reason, or the emergency should happen after regular office hours, I further authorize __(firm name here)__ to take my pet(s) to the nearest emergency veterinarian clinic __(name of clinic here)__ which can render assistance.

Signed: _____ Date: _____

Printed name: _____

Address: _____ City: _____

Pet(s) full names: _____

_____

_____

_____

——————————— *Your pet deserves the best.* ———————————

Fluffy wanted to catch butterflies,
She gave it many tries,
Each day's end came the same,
She only succeeded with flies!

6   The Interview

Before you ever go on your first interview you should have some basic information about your customer already written down on the background history sheet, pet personality profile, and veterinarian release form. I always try to have as much information as possible garnered in advance so I look knowledgeable during the interview itself. At the least, you know the customer's name, address, city, telephone, date and time of the interview.

It is good to add as much to this information as possible over the telephone. Knowing the pet's name and sex is important so that you can address the pet by name upon arrival at the interview. This is certainly possible with one or two pets. When the customer tells me over the phone that they have four, six, eleven, or thirteen pets, I do not even attempt to get names and sexes of any of the pets. Most of the information you obtain on the telephone will be determined by the personality of the caller. The more outgoing the personality, the more helpful the information.

The Tools You will Need

The interview and the job of sitting both require some basic tools. For the interview, you need to walk into the prospect's home with all your supplies in one container. When I began my business I used a plain zippered bag. Whatever your choice of container, you should have some paper clips, a felt or ink pen for filling in the forms, a picture of your pets if you have any, and twenty business cards. You want one background history sheet, a pet personality profile sheet, a veterinarian release form, and some blank paper for notes. In addition to these items, you want to carry two each of references, peace of mind, fee schedule, biography sheet, and tips for a happier vacation sheet.

In your car you should have a map, a flashlight, and instructions (if given) on how to find the home. You have two of most forms because if the prospect says the next-door neighbor would be interested in your service also, you want to leave her an extra set for the neighbor. The other items will be explained as we delve further into the chapter.

Nothing you will do in the course of your business is as critical or as important as the preliminary interview. Your income, your job, your reputation, and your future repeat business all depend upon your actions during this initial session.

I don't want to make you nervous or afraid of making this first interview, but I do want to stress that if you do not book the business on this first interview, you have only yourself to blame. Think about this for a moment. What other sale of any product or service depends totally upon your actions? Encyclopedias, insurance, cars, funeral plots, cosmetics, or any other product you can think of can all be put off till next week, month or year. You don't have to buy anything from anyone. You can procrastinate. This potential customer of yours, however, has only limited choices. It's going to be you, the kennel, or the kids next door. The potential customer is going to take some action! You want this person to decide in favor of your services.

This single step of the business cycle is so vitally important that I am going to devote a considerable number of pages to just how to act, what to say, and how to control the interview process. You need to read and reread this particular chapter. It is the vital heartbeat of your business. Mentioning things like shaking the customer's hand and handing out a business card may seem too obvious to mention. Believe me, I am not trying to insult your intelligence. I have seen so many poor presentations of services that I am amazed at the number of things that can be forgotten during this nervous time. Most things that you refuse to buy can be traced to their presentation. What you don't understand, you don't want. Your presentation must be thorough.

Introduction

You have selected a time to visit the prospect. The time has been mutually agreed upon. The prospect has no idea how long this interview will take, but you do. It should take no less and no longer than a half hour. A half hour is all that is needed to get all the information, wrap up the details, and make the sale. Yes, it is a sale! The customer will not know it is a sale, only you will know that. If you conduct the interview properly, the customer will find the decision-making process a natural one, not contrived. The customer will automatically make the right choice, without hesitating to think or worry about any details. You are in command; you will conduct the interview. You will guide the customer through every phase and treat each interview as though you have been through the act hundreds and hundreds of times, even on your very first one! Yes, I was scared on my first interview too, but the key to overcoming fear is preparation. Know your material and fear will sit in the back of your mind—not the front.

Incidentally, never, ever, be late for an appointment. The impression left in the prospect's mind if you are late is that you are careless or sloppy. You can arrive a half hour early (I have) rather than being five minutes late. I always apologize for being early by saying, "I didn't know how long it would take to get here, so I am sorry to be so early, but I just hate being late." Customers will truly appreciate your thoughtfulness.

The secret to being early, in some cases, is to find the home prior to the call. Many times I have driven out, flashlight in hand, in the dark of night, to find the exact location, note how long it takes to get there from home, and then return at the appointed time. Until you are thoroughly familiar with your area, this may be the only way to assure yourself of being on time. If you have lived in your town for twenty years and know the location of every house on every street, you are way ahead of the game.

There is one final advantage to being early for an appointment. You will usually be shown into the home and allowed to wait while the prospective customer is getting ready for your visit. This gives you time to take note of the surroundings, possibly play with the pets you are intending to sit and gain some information in advance of the actual interview.

I am going to describe this interview in terms of how I did it from the beginning. I include a lot of detail that you may wish to skip. I strongly suggest that you adopt all the relevant material for your presentation. Your wording won't be the same as mine, but the order of presentation is important.

You start each interview casually and build to a climax. For your first ten interviews, try to remember to smile. You'll find yourself grimacing at times because you are trying hard to remember all the details. Take comfort in the fact that the customer has never heard this presentation before. How can you make a mistake? Nobody but you knows what you are going to say. If you forget some part, get lost in thought, or falter in any way, just sit back, relax, and smile. The customer will smile too. It's contagious!

Don't rush through the interview. Everybody likes talking about his or her pets. If your first few interviews have to take an hour, nobody will notice except you. Relax, this is going to be fun.

I ring the doorbell. I have no idea who is going to answer the door so I wish to be professionally prepared to introduce myself by handing a card to the person who answers. I state my name and that I am the pet sitter. I want to keep stressing that the name of my company is of no interest to anyone but me. I am the pet sitter. Everyone understands that. That is how I introduce myself.

The person who answers the door will invite me inside. I have never been asked to wait at any door, except by a dutiful child who was instructed by parents to keep strangers out of the home. I am always invited in because I have an appointment. I am not selling anything at this point; I simply have an interview. An interview sounds much nicer than a sales pitch, but believe me, that is exactly what I am going to give this prospect!

How I open the conversation with the prospect determines who will control the interview. Let me state that again—because of its importance to your success:

How you open the conversation determines who will control the interview.

If a prospect is allowed to ramble through the interview, asking all sorts of questions (in effect interrogating you), you will appear on the defensive and off-balance. Football games, battles, and ultimately wars are never won by being defensive. Everything is won by being on the offensive.

I begin the conversation with an ice-breaking statement:

"Good evening Mrs. Smith (I shake hands with her). My name is Bill Foster; I am the pet sitter you spoke with on the telephone the other evening. I have some literature I would like to show you. Could we sit at your kitchen table? (After being seated.) Before we get started I want to give you this list of character, personal, and business references. These folks have known me personally for the past years and I want you to feel free to call any or all of them to discuss my integrity. My bank reference is also listed. I have been banking with that firm for the past ten years."

The prospect will usually put the form down without a further glance. Now I begin to control the interview. I lead off with the next question before the prospect can ask anything else. If I have already seen one or more of the pets, I say something nice about the pets. Something such as, "Mrs. Smith, Misty here seems like a very gentle little girl. Is she an only child?" When I make these comments, I make them questions.

I always ask questions that can be answered simply, without much thinking by the owner. Questions that can be answered either "yes" or "no" are very good. As I ask the questions, I slowly remove the background history sheet, pet personality profile, and veterinarian release form from my folder and jot down the answers. There is a space on these forms for all the questions I am asking. I keep the questions light and airy for the first five minutes.

At this early point in the conversation, I casually happen to remember a photograph of my pets that I carry in my folder. I pull out the photograph and ask the prospect if she would like to see a picture of my children. We happen to own three poodles; black, white, and brown. We have a cute snapshot of all three lined up in a row. The presentation of this picture never fails to get "oohs" and "aahs" from the audience. Why do you need a picture of your pets? Would you buy a baby book written by a spinster? Would you fly in an airplane with a flight instructor who had never flown? Would you believe a word in this book if I weren't currently doing what I am telling you?

If you own pets, don't go to this first interview without a picture! It is vitally important to increase your credibility and enhance your image in the eyes of the prospect. While we're at it, here's another never: never, ever, comment on the home you are visiting. Even if you live in modest surroundings and you walk into a palace, make no comment. You may think that you are complimenting someone by saying what a lovely home the person has, or what a beautiful view from the window. What you are doing may possibly be perceived as a cat burglar stalking the game! You never want to act impressed, overwhelmed, in awe, or amazed at what you see. From the very plain to the very opulent, you will see it all. Your attitude should always be that you have seen it before and will see it again. Cordial, neutral, and friendly is your approach.

I have made "small talk" for the first five minutes. It is now time to go for the sale. I take out the tips for a happier vacation sheet and hand it to Mrs. Smith. I tell Mrs. Smith that I have created this little list as a "reminder" for folks. It is really handy in helping people think of things most commonly forgotten before departure. Now I take out the peace of mind sheet. I tell Mrs. Smith that I have a twenty-two point inspection program for each time I visit her home and pets. I take out the biography sheet and hand that to Mrs. Smith. I tell Mrs. Smith that this is more information on my service. Mrs. Smith now has four sheets of paper and will likely stack them together and put them aside. Mrs. Smith will make a comment like, "My, you certainly are well organized."

At this point I pick up my pen, put the background history sheet, pet personality profile, and veterinarian release form in front of me and say: "I like to use a check list format so that I can assure myself I have asked all the questions that need answering. If you don't mind, I would like to go through my list and make certain we don't overlook any vital information. Let's begin with some background on Misty."

Mrs. Smith agrees and usually tries to scrutinize the sheet I am writing on, wondering what in the world all those little lines and spaces are for. I begin with the pet's name. A "Misty" to me could be a "Mistee" to Mrs. Smith. Owners are very touchy about the spelling in a pet's name. I ask the age, sex, and type of breed (if it isn't obvious). A mixed-breed cat may be a mixed-breed cat to me, but if it has a touch of Persian in it, Mrs. Smith will tell me. I write down "Persian" if that's what Mrs. Smith tells me.

I then ask Mrs. Smith the day and month Misty was born. I tell her it's not important for the record, but since Misty probably doesn't get much mail, I want to send Misty a birthday card on her proper birthday. Owners get very happy to hear the pet is going to receive recognition in this nice way. This birthday card is another subtle plug for your services.

I ask Mrs. Smith if Misty is fed morning and evening. Most cats and dogs under twelve months of age are fed twice a day. I check the appropriate box. The same question is then asked about wet and dry food, and the amount. At this point in the interview, Mrs. Smith jumps from her chair and starts toward the kitchen to demonstrate the quantity of food and where it is kept. I ask Mrs. Smith if we can defer the tour until we have completed all the questions and then I would enjoy seeing where everything is kept. If I leave the table with Mrs. Smith, and go to the kitchen, I have lost control of the interview. Besides, there are a lot more questions that need answers before we tour the home.

I ask about the toys, treats, and separate bowls. (This only applies if there is more than one pet in the home.) I ask if Misty is kept inside or has a pet door to allow her to go outside if she wishes. I circle the appropriate response. I repeat this process for as many pets as there are going to be in my charge. If Mrs. Smith has a dog, but she is going to take it along with her on the trip, I will take down no information whatsoever about that pet because it isn't going to be in my care.

Once I have covered every pet through the pet personality profile, I move to the background history sheet. The only information I have so far on this sheet is in the first four lines. In many cases the work phone number is missing so I ask for that. I inquire what vet clinic the family uses for the pets. Is there a specific doctor? In the event of an emergency, is Mrs. Smith going to be at a telephone number where she can be reached?

I stress here that I would only call Mrs. Smith in the event of something catastrophic such as an earthquake. I pick some remote possibility as the cause of my concern. In the midwest, it's a tornado. In the east, it's a blizzard that cuts off all power. In the south, it's a hurricane. In the northwest, it's a winter ice storm. Pick an event that is not likely to occur. Your real concerns are more likely to happen. What about burglary? What if the cat gets lost? What about a broken window? Almost anything can happen and you need to inform the owner, or someone close to the owner, so action can be taken. I then ask for the telephone number of a neighbor/friend/relative using the same reasoning as above. You can even volunteer to call them with a progress report on the pets. It is much more likely, however, that the owner will call you if she is concerned. Here's a real-life example of why you might want to call the owner during the sitting.

We had a ten-day assignment during the dead of winter. The weather had been beautiful up to the time of the owner's departure. Seven days into the sitting, the worst rainstorm of the season came in with a roar.

The temperature dropped to freezing at night and the snow level slammed down to 2,000 feet. Both dogs were kept on an outside patio and we were concerned for their health. A case of pneumonia is not good as an inducement for future bookings! There was an unlocked gymnasium room which had indoor-outdoor carpet. We thought the dogs would be much warmer and safer inside the snug comfort of the sealed room.

We didn't want to put the pets inside against the owner's wishes, so we called them at their vacation spot and informed them of the situation. The owners were extremely grateful for the call and completely agreed with our decision. Everyone was happy and the pets stayed dry and healthy. You could use a real-life situation like this to explain your need for telephone numbers, but it is much better to keep it on the mythical side and leave the owners without worry or stress.

Now I am ready to complete the "yes" and "no" check list. It is interesting to note that at this point that Mrs. Smith has relaxed and usually is more comfortable in her chair. As we get deeper and deeper into the conversation about Mrs. Smith's cat, I can actually see the tension fading away from her face. It is fun to watch the prospect go from apprehension and worry, to relaxation and relief, all within the span of a half hour. If you do your interviews correctly, it will happen every single time.

Is the yard fenced? Does Misty have a pet door? Does Misty like to be brushed? If Misty is to be brushed, I remind Mrs. Smith to leave out the pet brush. Does Misty walk on a leash? Most cats don't but you never know in advance. If Misty does walk on a leash, I remind Mrs. Smith to leave the leash out, too, just like the brush. Does Mrs. Smith have enough food on hand? Is Misty on any medication now? If so, I defer the question to a later time, I want to finish the check list right now. Are any plants going to need watering? If so, Mrs. Smith needs to leave the watering can out for me. Is there a sprinkler system? (I take a look at where the faucets are later in the tour of the yard.) Bring in the newspapers? Mail? Sign for packages? Change the lighting?

A good light to leave on for the pet is a stove light in the kitchen where most pets usually eat. It is low wattage and doesn't give off much heat. I suggest a rotation system of turning some lights on and off on different evenings. For example, the first night I may leave the porch light on, and the next night, a lamp in the front room, just so it always appears someone is home. Many people have lamps on timers which solves the problem entirely.

Answer the telephone? Most people have planned for messages. There are some folks though who may want you to check the recorder and call them with messages. If you do this from the customer's phone, it costs you nothing.

A security system? If Mrs. Smith has a security system in her home, then I must learn the code or have a special code of my own to use. Incidentally, in many push-button alarm systems owners can program separate codes for special events. Our favorite code is the last four digits of our telephone number and the password "dog" or "cat," depending upon the owner's pets.

Inspecting the security system will be done during the tour of the home.

Where is the garbage can for putting litter box wastes? What day do I set out garbage cans for collection? Is this the first time Misty has been left alone in the house overnight? If yes, I may face a real problem. Not eating is common. Chewing furniture is common. I might as well prepare Mrs. Smith for some adverse reactions by Misty if she is allowed free reign of the house for the first time. (One cat we sat for chewed a whole liner out of the bottom of a queen-sized bed mattress!)

Is anybody going to be on or in the property during her absence? This is important to clarify. I usually say, "Mrs. Smith, I want you to think long and hard about this question. If you say nobody will be here then if I see anyone, I should call the police, right?"

I had one customer readily agree that nobody would be around, and then within ten seconds she remembered the gardener on Friday and, oh yes, her daughter on Wednesday. One family even forgot that a crew of six gardeners were putting an entire new lawn onto the front and backyard! You don't want to have relatives arrested. On the other hand, you don't want to wave "hello" to a burglar you pass on the way out! If Mrs. Smith tells me nobody will be in the home but me, then I write in the blank space "nobody—call police." This reminds me that I am the sole caretaker and to check the security on each and every visit.

When did Misty go to the vet's office last? I give Mrs. Smith some vague parameters here. A couple of weeks? A couple of months? While Mrs. Smith is trying to remember the date of Misty's last vet visit, I slip the veterinarian release form to the top of my papers and fill in the heading with the name of Mrs. Smith's veterinarian. (I learned that name from one of the first questions on the background history sheet.) At the bottom of this same form, I also write in the proper names of each of the pets.

After Mrs. Smith tells me the date of her last visit to the vet's office, I place the veterinarian release form in front of her and say:

"Mrs. Smith, I'm certain that while you are gone Misty will be just fine. However, since Misty is not our pet, we need a veterinarian release form to be able to take Misty to your vet if something were to happen. We keep these forms on file so there is no question of getting quick care for Misty."

Mrs. Smith signs the form. I always place my pen in front of the customer so the customer doesn't have to look for a pen to use.

I am ready to finish my background history sheet. In fact, I am just about done with all writing. At this point, I am going to give Mrs. Smith the fee schedule, just as soon as I find out the times and dates. Here is a typical conversation.

> Me: "What day are you actually leaving?"
> Mrs. Smith: "On the twenty-sixth of June."
> Me: "Are you leaving early or late on that day?"
> Mrs. Smith: "We're leaving in the morning, at seven that day."
> Me: "Misty needs to be fed twice a day. My service would begin on the first evening, the twenty-sixth. Correct?"
> Mrs. Smith: "That's correct."
> Me: "You will be home the evening of July third so that means my service ends the morning of July third?"
> Mrs. Smith: "Yes, that's right."
> Me: "Mrs. Smith, here's another advantage of our service. Take these two extra cards with you on your trip. We have an unlisted number so please don't lose them. You can call us any or every evening, if you wish, and find out how Misty is doing. Also, if you decide to come home early or stay longer, just give us a call. You won't be charged for any call we don't make."
> Mrs. Smith: "That's great!"
> Me: "By the way, here's my fee schedule. When you return home you will find a letter on how Misty did while you were away, along with a statement and an envelope. You can just mail me a check."

At this point you would probably expect Mrs. Smith to examine the fee schedule, find out how much that period of time was going to cost, and make some comment. Wrong! The great majority of all your customers will glance at your fee schedule for less than five seconds. Here's something to burn into your memory to be recalled during your interviews: "The only person in the room concerned with price will be you."

The owner is not concerned with price. The owner is concerned with the safety, security, comfort, and happiness of the pets. You are the only person who thinks about price. Anybody who is really concerned about costs will ask you the cost on the telephone prior to the interview. Remember to always discuss costs on the telephone prior to going out on any interview unless the number of pets makes costs impossible to judge until the interview itself.

A word about large pet collections here. When a caller tells me over the phone that they have seven, eleven, thirteen, or more pets, it is totally impossible to predict a total cost for the sitting over the telephone. In order to give the caller some basis for consideration, you can state that your cost for four pets is "XX" and this would certainly exceed that amount. This immediately disqualifies any person who was expecting to hear a lesser sum of money than your normal charges for four pets.

To avoid a lengthy interview where price may be a stumbling block, I do the following. After the first five minutes of initial conversation I ask the owner, "Why don't you show me all you would like done during a typical visit and then I can tell you if we can do it and what it would cost." The owner then shows me what needs to be done and I begin assessing the cost as we go through the routine. Once the demonstration is complete, I sit back down at the table and calculate what I will charge for that particular situation. Twenty-five dollars for the first visit of the day and fifteen dollars for the second visit are not uncommon sums where many pets are involved in the household. Once I give the owner the exact quotation, and the owner agrees that sum is acceptable, we proceed with the interview. Once again, cost is not the issue. Cost has been resolved.

You won't believe that cost will not be a factor until you have completed your first five interviews, but you will then understand it is true. Price will only be a topic of conversation if you talk about it. The customer will put the fee schedule down along with the other four papers and will not look at it again, until you are gone. Trust me on this one point. Do not discuss fees at all on a normal interview. The customer won't if you don't.

Once I have gotten Mrs. Smith to tell me the start and finish date of the sitting, the job is mine. The interview is finished. You see how easy it is? Do you see the natural progression of questions all leading up to the close of the sale? There appears to be no huge decision for the owner to make during the interview, just a series of small decisions which are easily understood.

The last question I need to ask while still seated at the table is who referred Mrs. Smith to me? In most cases I cover that question during the telephone conversation, prior to the interview, but if I forgot, I ask it now and write it down. It will be important at a later date because you are going to reward business owners who send you referrals.

A tour of the home now follows and I pause at each point along the way to make notations of vital things I am told. Some notes I put in the margins where appropriate, some notes must be made on the extra pad I brought along for that purpose. I note where the food is kept and what quantity and portion of each should be fed and at what times. I note where the "special toys" are located so I can assure the customer that I will be playing with them and the pet. I ask where the meals are served, how far apart the dishes should be set, and make notes on that. I find out where all the plants are located and which should be watered and which should not. I have Mrs. Smith show me the litter box (or boxes) and ask how often she would like the entire litter changed. I see how many outside doors are in the house, how each can be checked, and which should be locked at all times.

A word here on security. Here is a statement I make to reassure the owner that the house will remain intact while she is gone: "Mrs. Smith, I would appreciate it if you would lock every single door, window, sliding door, etc. before you leave. Shut every door in the house you don't want Misty going through. Shut all cupboards and cover any furniture that Misty might scratch. In return, I will make certain that, until you return, everything stays just as you have left it."

This statement makes it perfectly clear to Mrs. Smith that I intend to touch nothing and that I will see things stay in order.

I want to find out where the can opener is located (if wet or canned food is going to be used) along with a rag or dishcloth which I may need to mop up water spills. I mention carpet spot remover which should be left out in case of accidents. I need to know where the watering can is and what it looks like. In locations where bottled water is popular, many people prefer pets to have bottled water instead of tap water. I find out if there is a preference for special water.

If there is medication to be administered, I need to be shown how, when, and how much. Finally, I want to tour the outside of the home and inspect the yard area. When I walk outside to the yard, I take my paperwork with me because I am going to depart from there. After the tour of the yard is completed, the interview is finished. I look at the sprinklers, garbage cans, and learn the security system. I examine the yard to see if the pets can escape the play area. Most everyone will have some area of the yard that the pets prefer to use as a bathroom. I need to know where that area is located. I need to determine for myself if I can safely let out the pets without worrying about them going under a fence and then having to chase them down the street.

When I finish touring the yard, I thank the customer for the interview, and ask for the key. I always try the key in the lock to make certain it works and is the correct key. (Yes, I have been handed wrong keys by mistake.) I reconfirm the dates and times from beginning to end so there is no doubt in my mind that the information is correct.

Did you notice how often during the interview I used Mrs. Smith's name? People like to hear the sound of their own names. Use the customer's name often during each visit. Remember to say good-bye to each of the pets—by name. This is important because the pets are truly your clients. It is a nice touch to remember the names. If you cannot readily recall the names, glance back at your notes; the names are written down there.

Finally, here are some rules that should go without saying. I will say them anyway for extra emphasis:

Never, ever, smoke in front of a customer. Never smoke in a customer's home when they are gone, even if the customer smokes. How would you feel if you burned something by accident?

Never, ever, show up for an appointment with liquor on your breath. Never have even one glass of wine or one bottle of beer prior to an interview.

Never, ever, discuss any of the customer's private business with neighbors. Don't tell the neighbors where your customer went or what the customer is doing—nothing. After all, if the neighbors are good friends with your customers, your customers would have told them already. If not, it's none of their business.

Never, ever, discuss any of the customer's private life, or habits, with any other customers. The best way to kill your business is to spread gossip among a group of people who may well know each other. You want to be known as a trustworthy, closed-mouthed person, who does the job well, and minds your own business.

Never, ever, knock your competition. You will notice that when I mentioned boarding dogs, I never said the word kennel. I never inferred my pets got fleas, eye infections, ear infections, or kennel cough from a specific place. I could have meant a private home for boarding. Even if you are asked your opinion on a boarding facility, you have no comment. You can recommend—but never tear down.

Reading this may give you the impression that it takes much more than half an hour to complete the interview. It doesn't. You will have some homes where the pets are always kept outside. This means you'll have no responsibility for the inside of the home whatsoever. You can just skip all the questions about lights, keys, plants, security, etc. Some customers won't want certain tasks performed. You skip those tasks. After all, the customer is free to use any portion, or all, of your available services. The choice is up to the customer. The price for the call is the same.

You should leave every interview with a good feeling. A feeling that you are performing a vital and needed service. Nobody but you in the whole world can do the job as well. If you have that attitude, you will see the customer's face go from anxiety and doubt, to relief and satisfaction, all during your half-hour visit. You'll get the job every time!

When you return home from this first interview, you need to make a heading on a file folder with the last name of the customer. In that folder you put the three sheets from your interview. The pet personality profile, the background history sheet, and the veterinarian release form are always kept in the customer's file.

Duddy sang opera, she knew three in a row.
Twenty-two minutes is a lot to know.

7 Doing the Job, Step by Step

Before you can begin a sitting for any customer, you need a check list to guide you through the procedure. A daily check list sheet you can use for this is shown at the end of the chapter. I suggest adding your letterhead to the top and using the form just as it is printed until you become experienced enough to modify it. I used a basic format for one year before I made any changes. The changes I made are reflected on this revised form.

The daily check list sheet is used for every visit you make to a customer's home. A new sheet for each day. The form has two purposes. First, it is a reminder of the twenty-two steps that may be necessary during each visit with the pets. Second, it is a record to be saved of your daily visit which can be used, if necessary, as proof of your performance. This is not a form to discuss with the customer or give to the customer. This is strictly an internal form which is kept, when completed, in the customer's file. At the end of each year, I throw away all completed forms. I suggest you print 100 copies of this form because you will need one form for each customer per each day of the sitting.

You will notice that the daily check list sheet has two lines numbered one and two. If you are going to make two calls per day, you will need both lines, one for morning and the other for evening. The twenty-two boxes on each side of the page correspond to the two lines above. The first box is for the morning visit, the second box on the same line is for the evening visit. For the rare customer that requires three visits per day, you either need a second form, or you simply add a third line and a third row of boxes. Three visits per day is not common enough to warrant designing a special form.

The two boxes in the top left corner labeled "yes" and "no" are to help you remember which jobs you must perform at each sitting. You mark on your check list before you arrive any items which are not to be performed. The "notes for the day" heading at the bottom is where you list those incidents which are worth mentioning to the owner in the letter you will prepare for the end of the sitting.

In addition to the daily check list sheet, you will need two other pieces of paper on your first call. Those two papers are the pet personality profile and the background history sheet. I put these two sheets back-to-back inside a glassine holder underneath a clipboard. I then have the customer's records on the bottom, and the daily check list sheet on top, all neatly stacked under the clipboard.

The Tools You Need

Before you go out on your first sitting job, you should put together a small kit that you will always carry in your car. This kit should become a permanent fixture in your car and you can replace parts as needed. Use a waxed paper shopping bag. If you can't find one, or don't own one, take a grocery store bag and line the inside with plastic. (This prevents the bag from becoming soaked during bad weather.) Your bag should contain the following items:

a flashlight which works
extra batteries for the light
a pair of gloves
a spatula
a dustpan
a box of small plastic bags
two hand towels
a box of of treats
a whisk broom
a roll of paper towels.

I will explain the needs and uses of these items as we go along. For now, just note the items and remember to take them with you on every sitting.

For this example we are going to imagine sitting which needs to utilize every single item on the daily check list. Many homes will not have security systems, houseplants to water, or newspapers to pick up. You must know how to follow the daily check list sheet, so we will begin with the assumption that this household needs every one of your services.

On arrival, you write down the time on the daily check list sheet. This is the first call of the morning. You take your clipboard along with the dustpan, spatula, two plastic bags, and the keys to the home. If I have any doubts as to the disposition of the pets, I take a dog treat with me. Every dog likes a treat. Even barking dogs stop to eat a treat.

You stop by the mailbox, pick up the mail along with the newspapers in the driveway, and walk to the front door. You see the red light glowing on the security panel and now you punch in your code to disarm the security system. You enter and place the mail and newspapers in the appointed spot. Check off your daily check list sheet that these first three tasks have been completed.

Now you find the pets and greet them. The first thing to do is empty and refill the water dishes. Make certain that the pets have enough water. Animals can live a long time without food, but can die without water in a very short time. Water is critical to survival. Never forget water. In fact, if there is any doubt in your mind about the water supply being adequate to the size of the pets, add another water bowl to make certain nobody runs out of water.

Food is the next item of business. Food and water are the most important items to pets. We do this before anything else because if you get interrupted, or (God forbid) you forget anything else, at the very least the pets have food and fresh water each day. You put the prescribed amount of food in each bowl. Let's start with the cat. The cat's bowl is always up high so the dogs cannot eat the food. Even if the owners normally feed the cat down on the floor next to the dogs, I suggest you feed the cat up on the counter, away from the dogs. Without the owners being present to act as monitors, the dogs may just decide to eat the cat's food first, instead of their own.

When the cat has fresh food, you feed the dogs. Put the bowls up high, away from the dogs, while filling them. Fill them with the prescribed amount. When you set the bowls back on the floor, feed the "chow-hound" first. Let me explain. In any family, one dog eats better than the other. From the first feeding it will become obvious to you which dog eats like a prisoner of war. Feed that dog first to keep it from eating the other's dinner. This is especially true of puppies. When I have a puppy and an adult dog,

I always feed the puppy first. The puppy will always eat better and faster than the adult.

Once both bowls are in place, stand over the pets. Make certain of two things. First, that each pet eats all the food. (Some pets won't eat unless you are watching them.) Second, see that each pet eats only its own food, not that of the others. When the pets are finished eating, go back to your daily check list sheet, mark the "meal eaten" box, and then remove the dishes to the safety of the counter or cupboard. You don't want to come back that evening and not be able to find the bowl. (Food bowls can become toys when empty.) Messy food bowls should be washed after every meal. I find paper towels handy to use for this purpose. Bring your own into the home if the customer has none.

Now, we have one dog that needs eye drops. Get that dog and the medication and put in the eye drops. Follow whatever directions the owner left you. Check that off the list. Put the food, medication, and bowls away and lock the cupboard. Again, check off the list. The next item on your check list says treats. Why treats now? Why not when you are ready to leave? One reason only. You need the pets occupied while you take care of the rest of your business. If you only have pets outside, and not much else to do, then you can save treats for when you leave. However, for inside pets, this is a good time.

You administer the treats and then look around to see if anybody has had an accident in the house. If so, use your handy spatula and dustpan to pick up the problem and dispose of it. You use the same procedure for the litter box. Here is where your plastic bags come in handy. If you find a problem, you need to take it to the outside garbage can. The house will smell like a sewer if you put it in the garbage under the sink and leave it for days on end. Never leave empty food cans or excrement inside a home. Use the outdoor garbage. If the family recycles, follow their directions for disposing of tins and other containers. Check the yard now for waste and clean that up too. If this happens to be garbage day, you set the garbage out by the street for pickup. Once all problems are attended to, you check off the cleanup item.

This is your first day so the next item of watering plants may not be necessary. If it is necessary to water, the watering can you talked about with the customer should be left for you on the counter. The hand towels you brought along are to wipe your hands after watering. The whisk broom you brought along is for sweeping up litter or dirt the pets left on carpeting, floors, or furniture.

If you need to turn on any outside sprinklers, this is the time to do it. This will give you about twenty minutes to water one area. Incidentally, the only outside lawn I ever volunteer to water is one which has a sprinkler system. Hand watering is much too time consuming and should constitute an additional charge to the customer if you consider doing it. I don't do hand watering of lawns because it is not profitable for me personally, compared to additional sittings. I do water outside potted plants as part of my regular service. In this case, if there are outdoor plants to water, do them about every third day.

It is now playtime. Depending upon the items you need to do on each sitting, you have between ten and fifteen minutes for play and/or walks. Most dogs who have access to a yard via a dog door don't need many walks. On the other hand, dogs confined to a small area (such as a laundry room) will need exercise. You need to walk them. Get out the leashes and collars (if the pets are not wearing collars already) and attach them.

Never, ever, walk a dog anywhere outside a fenced yard without a lead. You cannot take a chance on the dog being hit by a car, running away, or just chasing a cat across an open field. You are responsible for that pet. You don't want the pet out of your sight while outdoors in the open. Keep every pet on a leash anytime it's outside the home and you will have no worries. I usually walk for about five minutes in one direction and then return. Down to the end of the road, out across the field, about ten minutes in total is enough. You can vary the time to fit your schedule.

Upon returning to the house, make certain the dog's feet are clean so he won't track mud onto that oriental rug in the hallway! This is not a big problem in dry weather. Last winter I walked a dog into a hard-dirt field (at least I thought it was hard dirt) and we sank up to our ankles and paw-tops in mud and it took me over twenty minutes to clean myself—then the dog. What a mess!

A few words about dog walking. You are the pet sitter. You are not a dog trainer or a dog exerciser-person. Some owners try to take advantage of your service by asking for the impossible. You cannot drag a dog down the street, choking it by a taut lead, and then wrestle your way back to the home. If a dog strains at the lead and hurts your hands, wear gloves. That's why the gloves are brought along. Many owners never walk their dogs but decide it would be a good idea since you volunteered. I now utilize an entire page disclaimer which states those dogs we will walk and those we won't. There are other conditions you should consider which may modify your walking habits as well.

In my area we have temperature inversions which make walking unhealthy (due to smog) for humans and pets alike. I don't walk dogs under those conditions. I didn't include my one-page disclaimer in this book because you will have to decide for yourself what circumstances determine whether you will or will not walk a dog. Your physical condition, age, local weather conditions, and the time of year will dictate what constitutes your walks. Experience will become a great teacher and you will quickly recognize certain breeds of dogs that are harder to walk than others.

Finally about walks, use good judgment in walking overweight dogs that are not in good physical condition. A dog who spends all it's time indoors eating too much food and getting fed snacks too often is not a good candidate to begin a rigorous program of twice-a-day marathon walks. Suggest to owners that, until a dog's stamina is built up, it may be advisable to limit the length of each walk. You're now finished with playtime and walks and you check off those two boxes.

If a dog enjoys being brushed, now is the time to brush the dog. It is also time for hugging and holding; the loving time. Playtime and loving time are two separate things because many pets don't play but do like to be held and loved. Older cats are a good example.

It is time to take a tour through the home and check all the doors and windows. You only need to do a physical inspection of the doors and windows the first time you are in the home. On following visits, you can just jiggle the handles to make certain that all are locked. You will be amazed at how many owners leave doors, windows, garage side doors, sliding glass doors, and such unlocked by accident. The reason is that last-minute rush to remember all the things to pack, take, and stuff into the vehicle. Little thought is given to whether that side door was actually locked. Usually you will find one or more areas unlocked or open on your first pass through the home. Make certain you lock these doors and see that they cannot be opened from the outside. Once your tour is over, check off internal and external doors.

You can change the lighting (as we discussed in an earlier chapter) by switching from a hall light to a bathroom light to a bedroom light. Any room that cannot be seen directly from the outside is a good one to leave lit. If the bathroom window is opaque, that is a good room. If you were a burglar, would you want to enter a home where a light is on in a room you couldn't see into? No. That's what you want—some protection for the home. Once the lighting is changed, or at least checked, make certain all unnecessary lights turned on by you are shut off. Some lights are left on by mistake by the owners. Oven lights, makeup mirrors, closets, store rooms, and cellars are common areas of customer forgetfulness. Check this item off your list.

You are now ready to leave. The most important item comes next. Make certain that all the pets are where they are supposed to be. Sound odd to you? Many times I have gone out for the mail only to find that a dog is following right in my footsteps. This was in my own home, fortunately, so I remembered to let her back in. You cannot forget the pets and lock them outside if they are supposed to be inside. The reverse can also be true. If you have more than three pets in the home in your care, take a head count to be certain everybody is there.

Get your supplies bag and put back all the things you have taken out during your visit. If you used a flashlight to look into the basement, make certain it's back in the bag. If you took off some personal jewelry to wash your hands, make certain you have that back on. If you used your own paper towels, put the roll back into the bag. Put your sack near the front door and get ready to leave. Your last duty inside the house is to close any door that may have been opened by you. As a good rule, I try to use only one door in each house, rather than opening them all up. That way, when I get ready to lock the place up, I know that I have only used one door and don't have to check four or five others.

All of these tasks will eventually fall into a set routine. You will find yourself doing things in certain ways that form a pattern. Once you have visited a house two or three times, your routine is set and it becomes very easy to accomplish all of your tasks more quickly. The first visit is always the most complex and confusing.

Once out the front door, you arm the home's security system. If it arms properly, then you can lock the front door. Put all your things back into the car and you are almost ready to leave.

The last item on your daily check list sheet is to glance back over the twenty-two items and make certain all have been done. If you have any doubts, go back and check. It isn't worth worrying about later. My wife has left her purse on the counter top while distracted with pets. I have left my clipboard inside a home. Always remember to check for everything you brought into the home on the call. Now you are through. Write at the top of the form the time you are departing and the total amount of minutes spent in this customer's home. This record is kept for each visit. Make any appropriate notes on the bottom if you have not done so while you were inside the home.

Your daily check list sheet is important to you for another reason. You want to know the average length of each call because if you find you cannot get the job done properly in a half hour, then you may have to reconsider your fees for this particular home if you sit for them again.

My theory about fees for sittings is that long and short sittings will average themselves out. If you have one pet at each of two homes and the first home only takes twenty minutes and the second home takes forty minutes, then eventually, given enough customers, all sittings will equal out to an average amount of time within your normal price range.

I suggest keeping each day's daily check list sheet in a handy spot near the telephone so that you can get to it if the owner calls and wants information about the pets. You may think at first you can remember all the details that happened. You cannot. If you have more than four customers a day, they will all run together in your mind. Keep notes handy so you can look and sound intelligent and professional when the owner calls you. Believe me—they will call you to find out how the babies are doing.

This is the end of your first sitting. It probably appears, here on paper, to take hours. Actually, everything on your daily check list sheet can be completed within thirty minutes. Once you get into a rhythmic cadence, you can do it easily in twenty to thirty minutes without missing anything on the list. Every time you visit the same house, it gets easier because you know where everything is and what to expect from the pets.

When scheduling your day's rounds, you must allow for driving time. At best, this means thirty minutes for the sitting and ten minutes of driving. At worst it means an hour or thirty minutes of each. You can have a full day with eight calls, a hard workout with ten calls, or be getting rich with twelve calls! Anything more than twelve calls per day average and I find I begin to suffer from fatigue. There is the added factor of interviews. You may have to schedule five or more interviews into a week. Many of these interviews are going to have to be at night if both people in the household work all day. A night interview after a full day of calls can be draining. Scheduling can become an important process. More about that in a later chapter.

☑ - YES
☒ - NO

Daily Check List Sheet

Day of the Week _____ Date: _____

1. Time Arrived _____ Time Departed: _____ Total: _____ Minutes
2. Time Arrived _____ Time Departed: _____ Total: _____ Minutes

☐☐ Security Release   ☐☐ Sprinkler
☐☐ Newspapers   ☐☐ Playtime
☐☐ Mail   ☐☐ Walks
☐☐ Fresh Water   ☐☐ Brushing
☐☐ Food   ☐☐ Loving Time
☐☐ Meal Eaten   ☐☐ Check Internal Doors
☐☐ Administer Medication   ☐☐ Check External Doors
☐☐ Re-store Supplies   ☐☐ All Pets in Place
☐☐ Treats   ☐☐ Change Lighting
☐☐ Cleanup   ☐☐ Re-lock Area
☐☐ Water Plants   ☐☐ Security Restores

Notes for the Day: _____

_____

Owner's Name (Last): _____

Rocky was acclaimed for the burglar in the pool,
But adding the gardeners was against the rule!

8   Finishing Touches

Now we come to the part which I truly consider the frosting on the cake. You have done your sitting assignment. You have completed two, four, six, perhaps even ten days of duty at the customer's home. Everything is going well and the customer is expected to return the day after tomorrow. Tomorrow is the day that you want to leave the customer a statement for services along with an activity letter. Today, you must prepare both.

The activity letter is just an update bulletin on how the pets fared during the owner's absence. A sample activity letter is found at the end of this chapter. You want to make the tone of the letter upbeat, friendly, humorous (if you are so inclined), and positive. You don't want to fill this letter with minor or major tragedies, tales of woe, or regale the customer with what obnoxious beasts the "darlings" were while the customer was gone. Keep the note brief, friendly, and to the point. Remember, the customer doesn't care about your feelings. Only the feelings of the pet are important to the customer. Understanding that is what you are getting paid for.

This activity letter should be on your letterhead. Type or handwrite the message. You can look at the sample activity letter for ideas, but your letter, of course, must fit your particular situation on that assignment.

Statement for Services

This is the payoff. This is the part that makes everything else worthwhile. You are going to get paid good money!

The statement for services (at the end of the chapter) can be used as an example, just put the information on your own letterhead and insert your name under the "paid in full" line, right before the word sitter. Also, you want to add your name to the "note" section to tell the customer how you would like your check made out.

When you are first starting out, I doubt if you will want a checking account in your business name. If you don't instruct the customer on the statement as to how to make out your check, the customer will automatically assume you want it made out to your business name. If you don't have a business checking account, you cannot cash the check! To avoid this problem, make certain you look at the check prior to your departure from the customer's home (if paid then). Make certain the check is properly made out and can be readily deposited to your account.

You will notice that this is a very basic form: no invoice numbers, no dates of service, and no frills. You may feel free to add all the gingerbread you wish. Since the payment is not tax deductible for your customer, it is not necessary to be too fancy with the form. You won't need a copy for your records as you will utilize a different method of recording shown in a later chapter. All these statements and activity letters should be prepared the night before the sitting ends and left, along with the mail, at the customer's home on the last day of the sitting.

Keeper of the Keys

You have just gotten your first key from your first client. Where are you going to keep that key so you don't lose it, misplace it, or confuse it with other similar keys? The simplest and most inexpensive form of storage is in an egg carton. Take an empty egg carton and cut the top off so you are left with twelve small trays. I used an alpha lettering system first. I printed the letters in the bottom of each cup with a felt pen. I purchased inexpensive paper discs at a stationary store and attached one to each set of customer keys. On the background history sheet there is a space to mark which keys you are using for each customer. It is at the bottom right-hand corner of the form. The last item says "key pickup." In this space you write the coding you have assigned that particular key. Coding by letter or number is a simple method of keeping keys straight and works as a security measure as well.

Many customers think they are being helpful by putting their name and address on the keys prior to handing them to me. I always remove that information immediately. If I should happen to lose that key when getting out of my car, it is an open invitation to burglary. By using a code where only you know what the code stands for, you ensure that lost keys will cause no damage.

88 Finishing Touches

As you gain customers, you will gain more keys on a permanent basis. Within a year, you could easily have permanent possession of seventy keys. At present I use a cabinet at home which has sixty-six plastic pullout drawers which can be divided in half to make as many as 132 individual drawers. This is my permanent key file for all customer keys.

Activity Letter

Dear Mr. & Mrs. Murphy,

Just a quick note to let you know that Shawnee and Smokey were both very good while you were gone. Smokey didn't dig in the flower box at all! Surprised? Luckily, Shawnee didn't decide to take a dip in the pool either.

Both Shawnee and Smokey ate their meals every day and licked the bowls clean, so they were never without food.

Your gardener says that you need to call him when you get a chance because the algae is building up in the pool again. He said you would know about that and what to do.

Thanks for the opportunity of sitting with Shawnee and Smokey. It was a real pleasure and they were both a joy.

Please give me a call upon your return so that I know you got home safely.

Cordially,

Bill Foster,
Owners/Sitters

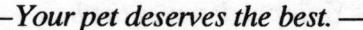
Your pet deserves the best.

Statement for Services

Customer Name: _____

Address: _____

City: _____ Zip Code: _____

Sitting service for ____ days at the rate of $_____ per day

    for a total of: $_____.

Sitting service for ____ days at the rate of $_____ per day

    for a total of: $_____.

Total now due: $_____.

Paid by check on: _____ . (date)

Paid in full: _____ . (sitter)

Note: Please make check payable to: _____

Thank you very much. We appreciate your business and look forward to serving you again, in the near future.

—————————*Your pet deserves the best.*—————————

Kong loved Tabby, of that there was no doubt,
All other cats Kong turned into a rout!

9 Supplementary Sales Ideas

There are many ways that you can get brilliant ideas and small flashes of genius when it comes to your own business: listening to a radio while you drive, glancing through your local newspaper, or even watching television commercials (believe it or not). All of these can give you new ideas to make your business more personalized, more tailored to your customer's needs, more localized to the area you live.

The local paper in my town was running a short spot on December 22 called, "What I most want for Christmas." The paper invited local residents to make comments to use as items of interest for the paper. Not one to miss a chance for free publicity, I submitted the comment, "What I most want for Christmas is to sit with as many pets that day as possible and make them happy!" Crass and commercial? You bet! I'll take free advertising wherever and whenever I can get it.

In your part of the country there must be parades, picnics, junior league, women's league, garden clubs, kennel clubs, welcome wagons, founder's day, chamber of commerce events, and all sorts of special holidays particularly aimed at your city. Take advantage of all these opportunities to volunteer to work with the clubs and associations. You make valuable contacts and can distribute your business cards to everyone you meet.

The following ideas are just some of the many things you can do to help your business thrive. You can add new ideas to this list almost on a weekly basis. Best of all, most of these ideas don't cost you any money.

Junior Achievement

There are rare instances when you can promote your own business and commit a helpful civic act at the same time. Junior Achievement provides one of these double opportunities.

Junior Achievement has four levels of programs which expose young people to the world of business. The first (and certainly most basic level) for which you can volunteer is the school program for fifth and sixth graders. You can call any office of Junior Achievement and volunteer as a business consultant. You pick a school near your home and commit yourself to four consecutive, weekly appearances for an hour each. You work with the class teacher giving the children structured, easy-to-understand material related to the business and the entrepreneurial world. In exchange, you also tell children what business you are in and can feel free to pass out your business cards, pens, pencils, scratch pads, or other promotional novelties you may use for your business.

If your own children are long-since grown and you can relate better to an older age group, you might just volunteer for the Project Business curriculum which is for seventh, eighth, and ninth graders. This program involves the same one-day a week visit, but is more advanced in thought. It includes role playing, economic simulations, written exercises, and lively discussions on current issues.

The children get exposure to the world of business and you accomplish two good deeds at the same time. All across North America there is a shortage of small business owner-volunteers to visit schools in each area and tell children about business. After all, teachers are in the world of academia, not business. Only you know about the world of profit and loss.

There is bound to be a branch of Junior Achievement located in or near your city. However, if you cannot find a local office, you can certainly write to this address for further information:

Junior Achievement Inc.
National Headquarters
45 Clubhouse Drive
Colorado Springs, Colorado 80906

I urge you to consider this worthwhile program as one of your first steps toward participation in community activities. You will find the experience both rewarding and enjoyable.

Gift Certificates

Gift certificates are something that everyone can use. You can advertise gift certificates in your local paper around the holiday season. More importantly, you can tell everyone you sit for that you have them available. Your gift certificate is available in any denomination. Think about that for a moment. Let's say a prospect knows that his next-door neighbor travels extensively. He would like to give this neighbor a gift of about $15 but he doesn't know how much your service is going to cost. That's fine with you. The prospect can apply that $15 toward the use of your service in the future.

This gift certificate accomplishes two things for you at once:

It gives you cash in advance for services at a later date.
It locks in a new customer for your services!

You should not bother making up gift certificates until the first person orders one. You can make a gift certificate a work of art with gilt-edged borders and multicolored print on the page, or it can be a simple handwritten note with the name of the donor, the amount of money, and the name of the recipient. The amount of money and energy you want to put into a gift certificate is strictly up to you.

Personally, I believe the best certificates are already designed and waiting for you at your stationery store. The stationer has gift certificates of all shapes and sizes on sale for a small price. It just isn't worth the trouble of designing a new format for such a little item. After you have been in business for a year and have extra money that you wish to spend, then I would recommend having a certificate custom made to fit your needs. Until then, a standard form from the stationery store is quite sufficient.

Remember to make the certificate good for up to one year (twelve months) from the date of purchase. Don't go over one year because you have to keep track of these certificates and remember how many were purchased and for what dollar amounts. Number each certificate and use a numbering system that is simple to remember. For future reference, you can list on a sheet of paper the name of the donor, the recipient, and the dollar value. Add the donor's name to your mailing list as a potential customer. Odds are that people who are thoughtful enough to give a gift certificate for pet sitting has pets of their own.

Thank You Ads

A good form of advertising is to thank customers for the success of your business during the past year. One of the cutest and most clever ways you can do this is to look through the records of all your sitting assignments for the past twelve months and pick out the pet's names. Use only the names in the ad, as in the following example:

"This past year has been an outstanding one for us at Paw Partners. We would like to thank those who made it possible for us to have such a great year. A special thanks to: Abbie, Amber, Cadbury, Dusty, Fred, Happy, Holly, Issac, Jasper, Keeters, Kitty, Muffy, Poncho, Rags, Reggie, Shawnee, Smokey, and Spot."

Go through your entire list and alphabetize it (in order not to offend the owners) and then list the name of every single pet you have been sitting during that past year. Can you imagine how happy the owners will be to see their pet's name in the paper? How often has your pet's name been in the paper? Probably never, like mine. The ad won't cost you that much money and the good will it generates will amaze you. The comments from your repeat customers are well worth the price. Try it!

Christmas Cards and Birthday Cards

For a small price this is another great advertising and revenue enhancing tool. Buy enough Christmas cards to cover every household you have been sitting for since you went into business. Regardless of the number of pets at the home, send one card to each household. Remember to buy a card for each business owner who recommends your service or allows you to have business cards in the store. Send those firms a card also.

Try to find a card that has animals on the cover. I found a card last year which had a dog and cat on the cover and both had fuzzy fur. Staple your business card to the inside blank side, sign the card with your name, and then print the name of your firm on the bottom. The second year you can splurge and buy cards printed with both your name and the firm name.

When addressing the card, make it out to the pets rather than the owners. For example it would be addressed to "Shawnee and Smokey" and then the address. The post office won't have any trouble delivering the card as long as you have the right address and mail codes.

You won't believe how many customers will call you to comment on your thoughtfulness. Owners are extremely happy when pets receive mail. Have you ever noticed the evening news often reports when a pet receives a credit card? Pets make good news and people love something different. Believe me, your card will get a place of honor on the fireplace mantle and be the source of much conversation.

The same is true for birthday cards. Here, instead of one card per household, send a card to each pet you have been sitting for. If there are three pets at a household, then mail out three cards on the appropriate dates. Remember, you got the birthdates from the owner when you initially filled out the background history sheet.

Speaking Engagements

This category is not for everyone. You must feel comfortable in front of an audience and be able to think on your feet or you will never enjoy this form of free publicity. If you cannot, or won't, speak in front of a group, just skip this suggestion entirely.

Now, if you are someone who can speak in front of a group, here is another great untapped treasure of free advertising. Women's groups, junior league, chamber of commerce, Kiwanis,

Rotary Club, Knights of Columbus, Lions, all these and more need guest speakers. Good guest speakers are hard to find. Interesting topics are hard to find. You can provide both of these. You have an interesting job and you can make your speech extremely topical as well. You can tell humorous anecdotes about things that happen to you during sitting assignments. You can mention funny things that pets do. You can talk about the great love and affection that most pets receive from owners. There are many, many topics you can find to comprise a half-hour or twenty-minute speech. There is only one thing you must avoid.

You never want to embarrass past or present customers by revealing anything that might make a customer feel singled out. If you want to mention a house where the dog deposited thirty-five piles on an oriental rug, it will be funny only if you misdirect the location and identity so the real owner cannot be pointed out by anyone. You don't want to get sued. You don't want to create ill will. You don't want to lose customers!

The best way to get a speaking engagement is to ask. It's that simple. You telephone the local club of your choice and ask to speak to the president. When you get the person on the phone, you ask for an appointment. In person, you explain your business and ask if you might be included in the speaking agenda for the coming months. Some people may want to see a copy of your speech prior to your delivery. That's fine. You should have your speech written out anyway. You can use the same speech at many functions because different groups have different memberships.

If you can find the free time between your busy sitting schedule and crowded interview schedule, public speaking is a great source of potential customers. Remember that after every speech, you have literature and cards available for those interested in taking them.

Security Firms

Somewhere in your area there are bound to be one or more security firms. In Los Angeles we have dozens. It is a good idea to meet these folks in person. You are going to be sitting for homes which have a security service. You want to be known by these people so that you won't be accidentally arrested some dark and rainy night as you are feeding Rover. Further, it is another excellent source of free advertising. Some people may ask the security service to do pet sitting duty. Most security services don't offer pet sitting as part of their routine, so you have no competition. Go into the headquarters of your local security firm(s) and introduce yourself, leave cards, and make friends. You can get many bookings from this one visit alone.

It's also a good idea to telephone your local police departments and tell them about your business. Some may want you to register with them so the department knows who you are. After all, your customers may have the house watched by the local police department during their absence and you don't want to be mistaken for a burglar.

Unlisted Telephone Number

This item is only worthwhile if you are starting your business and have an unlisted telephone number. We did. We have an unlisted telephone number and agonized over the thought that people couldn't find our number if the card was lost. What should we do? Then my wife hit upon a brilliant idea. Turn the disadvantage into a selling tool.

If you have an unlisted telephone number—don't list it. Instead, at the interview, tell the customer the following: "By the way, please don't lose my card because I have an unlisted telephone number. As I told you before, I have a very small, limited clientele and I chose not to be listed in the book." (Give the customer extra cards at the interview to take along on vacation so the customer can call you and check on the pets.) You will not believe the elite appeal of that statement! You will get funny looks from some customers but, on the whole, it really has proved to be a blessing in disguise. It makes your business card a more precious commodity.

A word of caution on this point of an unlisted telephone number. I hasten to add that I am the only firm that I know of in the United States using an unlisted number. Most pet sitters who advertise in the yellow pages think I am crazy to be unlisted. Most competitors think I must be starving for business without a listed number. I have no measure of how much more business I might have if we advertised and were listed in the telephone book. It has worked thus far for us, that's all I can say. If you are already listed in the telephone book, it is certainly not worth the effort of taking your name out of the book.

The 3½-by-2-inch Power

The most successful salesperson ever invented was not a person at all. The most successful sales tool is the 3½-by-2-inch business card. You have probably seen so many business cards in your life that you have forgotten the power that exists in that little card. Have you ever met an Asian business person and noticed that the first thing that person did was to press a business card into your hand? Asian business people are continually using what we seem to have forgotten years ago. Business cards in the hands of many people generate more business!

The most successful car salesman in the world attributed all his success to getting his business cards into the hands of as many people as possible. In the height of this salesman's successful days, he estimated that he went through as many as 25,000 business cards per year! Can you imagine that?

Always carry your business cards with you. Even when you are on a sitting assignment, you may be walking the dogs and meet neighbors. Give them a business card. You may be dining in a restaurant and somebody might casually ask what you do for a living—give that person a business card. Think about this.

You are given (or ask for) business cards hundreds of times during the year. Women store business cards inside wallets and purses. Men sometimes keep business cards in drawers or in business card boxes. It is not the immediate usage that you are looking for, it is more subliminal. How often in your life has someone said to you, "I wish I could find a real good . . ." You have replied, "Wait a minute. I think I have a card somewhere from a person who does just that very thing!"

You see, most people are just like you. Most people squirrel away business cards because someday they might just need them. That's what you are hoping for. Long-term business, far, far into the future, which springs to life from a totally unexpected source. At a nominal cost of about two cents each, what other advertising tool will you ever find that can reach so many people?

The Unsolicited Recommendation

An idea came to my wife one day while we were doing some routine sitting assignments. We were driving toward the next call when out of the blue she said, "Don't you wish pets could tell their owners what a great job we do for them? What if the pets read the owner a card which told them we did a good job?" I hadn't the slightest idea what she meant! She explained her idea to me further.

What we developed from that brainstorming is a card which looks, in size and format, like a wedding announcement. It is enclosed in a plain envelope, given out along with the customer's statement. We have written diagonally across the upper right-hand corner the words, "Please ask Rover to read this to you aloud." Inside is the unvarnished testimonial of her pet, Rover, telling Mommy what a great job Paw Partners has done for him!

> *"Paw Partners is really great!*
> *Have them come back and visit real soon."*
> *(signed)* **Your Loving Pet**

It never fails to provoke a laugh from the owners. We spent forty cents on each to purchase and print these cards. We feel the thoughtfulness (not to mention the laugh factor) is well worth the added expense.

Always be thinking about new ideas which can spice up your business and perhaps brighten your customer's day with a small chuckle. Here's another idea.

A Magnetic Attraction

I was looking for something homespun, inexpensive, useful, and worthwhile to give my customers. At the same time I wanted the usefulness to be much greater than my actual cost. I found just such an item, totally by chance, while walking through our local shopping mall one weekend.

The mall was having a handicraft festival with homemade items on display that had been created by senior citizens. We spotted some magnets that had common first names printed on each of them. Other magnets on the board had love, peace, and the standard fare written across each of them. My wife again had the flash of an idea. She inquired of the booth attendant if it were possible to get custom magnets with anything we wished painted on them. The lady informed us that her granddaughter was making the items and she would ask her and let us know. A week later the granddaughter called us and said she would get six samples ready for us to look over.

We selected the style which we liked best and asked her to make 100 of them for us. The magnets have the words Paw Partners painted in bright red letters with the telephone number written in black beneath them. At the bottom of each magnet is a three-toed paw print. We got the first twenty magnets within two weeks and started passing them out on each sitting assignment. As soon as we entered each new job, we would position one of these magnets on the refrigerator. These days, most everyone has some notes stuck to the family refrigerator.

We received nothing but favorable comments about the magnets and decided to see if it might be useful to give the magnets to the veterinarian offices where I had cards placed. Here, too, the magnets were warmly received. Every veterinarian has a refrigerator in their building and some veterinarians wanted more than one magnet. Receptionists at some veterinarian offices placed the magnet near the telephone. Pet shop owners wanted the magnets too. Groomers had refrigerators which could use magnets. In short, the magnets were a big hit. Our cost? Sixty-five cents per magnet. Cheap by anybody's standards. I suggest that you consider giving out some small token with each call if you find something, like the magnets.

Pet Food Lids

In many sittings for customers using canned (wet) food, we noticed that the customers didn't have any lids for the open cans. Where pets eat only half a canful of food, the uneaten half needs to be refrigerated. We were using aluminum foil, waxed paper, and small plastic bags to keep the open top covered. I found a company who sold plastic pet food covers. One size lid fit two sizes of cans. We ordered five hundred of these lids and had our name and telephone number printed in large letters across the face of the lid. Now when we enter a home which has no pet food lids, but has a need for refrigerating pet food, we leave a lid. Just another free service you can offer your regular customers.

Novelties like this can enhance your business by rewarding your customer with a fuller and richer service than your competition offers. I would much rather give the customer more than is expected than cheapen the service and offer less. Anything you can purchase which costs $1 or less per customer has a very inexpensive cost-to-customer ratio.

Quarterly Newsletter

Here is a format which combines several good ideas. First, it is a reminder to past customers that you are still interested in their pets. Second, it also serves as a tickler to prospects who merely inquired earlier. Third, it contains information that is of interest to each of the recipients because your topic is—pets!

A minor point of this mailing (but a major issue for you) is that you always include updated information about your own service. In the sample issue, at the end of this chapter, you will notice that I managed to get in four promotions for my own business. Why not? It's my mailing.

Where do you get the information for your quarterly mailings? You have a myriad of sources, including magazines, newspapers, vet offices, pet shops, and groomers. You save all the clippings you find regarding pets. Further, jot down any solid information you hear on television and radio. You borrow anything and everything that is not specifically protected by copyright. Another way to gain material is to ask permission to use articles you find published in pet magazines. I now receive ideas from my customers to include in upcoming issues. My customers save ideas and articles and these are a good source of news. My last issue was six pages of information. You want to keep your newsletter bright, breezy, upbeat, cheerful, and fun to read. I get compliments all the time on the issues. I am looking forward to the day when I find it necessary to publish a monthly newsletter!

Remember to print your telephone number along with your company name on every page of the newsletter so a prospect knows what number to call for more information about your service.

Supplementary Sales Ideas

Spring

Paw Partners
(213) 555-1212

This Year

Paw's Penny Post

Free Dog and Cat Food! You may have recently received in the mail an offer from a new brand of dog and cat food called *Perform*, made by a division of the Carnation Company. You can get a free sample of canned or dry food for your dog, puppy, cat, or kitten by calling: 1-800-000-0000. There is no obligation. We got our sample via UPS within six days and our dogs gobbled it down. The food is similar to other brands only has the appearance, size, and texture of the dry food.

Spring Break is Coming! Easter week is rapidly approaching and with it comes another busy season for us. If you and your family are planning to escape the city during the holidays, please let us know as early as possible so we may reserve the time to sit with your pets.

I didn't know that! Did you know that feeding your pets two, three, or four times a day with smaller portions of food is more preferable than one large meal each day? According to a recent veterinary study, digestion, disposition, and overall health are improved in pets receiving small, spaced feedings.

Expanded Area Service! We have extended our coverage area to include the cities of El Sequndo, Hermosa, Redondo, and Manhattan Beach. If you know of anyone in these areas who would like further information, please have them call us for a fee schedule and details.

———————*Your pet deserves the best.*———————

Paw Partners
(213) 555-1212

Spring   This Year

Paw's Pendix

Your Garden will Grow! Any cat lover has experienced the problem of cat urine upon plants. How can you keep your kitty (or your neighbor's) from tromping through flower beds and digging in potting areas? A great, humane method is to plant garlic in the area. Cats hate garlic and will avoid the area completely! Another method is to spread aluminum foil over any area you want protected. Cats don't like the sound their paws make when they walk on the foil and after two or three attempts, they will avoid that area too!

"Can You Help?" Department! As you may be aware, there is a great need for "in-home" boarding facilities in the area. Many people are simply more content knowing their pets will be cared for in a "home" environment. We get many calls, weekly, asking if we board dogs, cats, etc. If you are willing to board dogs, cats, etc., in your home and will incorporate them into your family life temporarily, call us. We will put you in touch with those folks who are asking us about boarding. All of these folks are willing to pay a daily fee for the kindness that is required. Please give us a call if you know of someone who would consider this. Thank you.

Bird Boarding Available! We now offer a very limited service of boarding for birds only. As birds are very social creatures, they enjoy the company of humans and like activity around them on a daily basis. When we board birds we incorporate them into our family life and give them entertainment to stimulate them. The rate for birds is $5.50 per cage, per day. You should remember that all birds need fresh water daily and they should be kept free from drafts at all times. If you lower your thermostat at night, your birds should be covered while they sleep.

———————*Your pet deserves the best.*———————

*Pet doors? Open windows? There must be other means—
Sheila only exited the house by breaking through screens!*

10 Bird Boarding

Bird boarding is one aspect of pet sitting that can become an exception to the rule about not taking any pets into your home. If you have a spare room (as we do) which you don't mind utilizing as a sitting room for birds, bird boarding can be a lucrative addition to your income.

Setting prices for bird boarding can take many forms. You can, for example, start out by saying you will charge by the type of bird. Then it will dawn on you that between canaries to parrots there is a lot of variation. How can you arrive at a flat rate? The best way is to take the lead from your local kennels. For birds, most kennels charge per cage, regardless of the number of birds in the cage. On occasion you will find that kennels will charge one price for a parakeet and a higher price for a military macaw, but generally price is set by the cage. Veterinarians, likewise, board birds and have standard fees. In my marketplace, the kennel rates per cage vary from a low of $4 per day to a high of $6 per day. I chose to charge a daily rate of $5.50 per cage to be just below the highest rate charged by the kennels. Why? Because in my own home I feel the birds get specialized attention that they won't get at the kennels.

The flier sheet at the end of this chapter shows that there are thirteen steps that you need to go through every single day with each bird. There could be as many as twenty steps to follow depending on the size, type, disposition, and routine of the birds involved. Most of the steps are so self-explanatory that it's unnecessary to detail each one here. There are some points, though, that we should discuss.

Delivery and Pickup

If the birds are not delivered to your home, and you must pick them up and redeliver them at the end of the boarding period, it is not unreasonable to charge a fee for this service. In my case I charge a flat $5 each way.

The reason for this seemingly high charge is that the trip is not really one way. You go out to pick up the birds for the first night. You have made a round trip. You go back to deliver them home. You have made another round trip. Each of these trips costs time and you must be compensated for your time. Remember—time is the only thing you have to sell. Service and time are your products!

Your charges for pickup and delivery of birds will have to be governed by two factors:

How far are you willing to drive?
How much time will it take?

Not publishing a price for pickup and delivery allows you the latitude to change the costs for any given situation. Here's a good example. I had a lady with two dogs and a cat who also owned a parrot. She wanted me to sit for a week with the dogs and cat and board the bird in my home. Now, do I really want to charge her transportation costs to and from my home when I am there to get the key for the sitting anyway? I decided to waive the costs and transport the parrot free. After all, I was getting $2.50 more per day for having the parrot at my home. Here's another case.

A senior citizen in an apartment complex doesn't own a car, but is going on a bus tour for an annual vacation. Would you charge her $5 each way to take her canary to your home? I didn't.

Supplies

Here again, just like pet sitting, it is up to the owners to provide everything that the birds are going to need during the owner's absence. If you are unfamiliar with birds, you may not realize (as many owners do not realize) that what appears like a lot of supplies, in reality, is probably not enough for the duration of the boarding period. I had a pair of parakeets that I boarded for ten days. Those two birds caused me to run to the pet store three times during the visit. First we ran out of treat, then we ran out of gravel, and then we ran out of seed! I added the costs (with a copy of the receipts) to the owner's statement for services, but I was still out the time involved in running the errands.

Make certain that the food, gravel, treat, and millet are sufficient for the length of the stay. There are some birds that cannot be provided for in advance. Birds like Toucans eat only fresh fruit. If the owner is going away for three weeks, the fruit would rot before you could serve it. In this case you will have to buy the fruit and charge accordingly.

The only thing you really need to buy for bird boarding is sandpaper. Many perches are positioned in cages so that excrement hits the perch. Also, when newspaper is used on the floor of the cage, the newsprint gets on the bird's feet and blackens the perch. A light rubbing with sandpaper removes most soiling and restores the grain of the wood. A good trick is not to use newspaper as a bottom liner for the cage. Instead, I use white paper towels and this keeps the perches from getting dirty in the first place. I keep a couple of rolls of generic paper towels in the bird room.

Playing with Birds

Make certain you ask the owner if the bird bites. The owner may never have been bitten, but that says little for your chances against an angry African gray parrot! I always use gloves the first day and then, depending on the outcome of the first encounter, I may remove the gloves for the rest of the visit. Some birds carry a virus which can get into your bloodstream through a bite. As a rule, if you receive a bite which breaks the skin, you should visit your family doctor and get a tetanus shot as a protection against infection—or worse. In light of this fact, gloves are good protection against a costly visit to your doctor.

Another good general rule for boarding birds is to leave the birds in their cages at all times, unless the owner waives your responsibility for the bird's safety. This is hard to do if the bird is especially cute and tame. Once out of the cage, the bird can fly in any direction and get hurt banging into glass, windows, mirrors, walls, etc. Even if the bird has clipped wings, it can fall to the floor in a thwarted flight attempt. Worst of all, the bird could go out a door and be gone forever.

Here in Los Angeles we have huge colonies which migrate from park to park, all descended from private pets which got away from owners. The southern fourth of the United States is unique in that it provides a haven for lost birds, and they can survive quite nicely without any human contact. Two blocks from my home is a square-block park which has a running waterfall and tropical plants. The parrot colony there thrives very nicely on dates, peppers, tangerines, seeds, greens, bananas, and crystal-clear running water! At any one time I can count at least thirty to fifty birds—each immigrated directly, or indirectly, through an open door in a private home!

What is a Day?

You will notice that the wording on the bottom of my flier is carefully phrased with the words "or any portion thereof." If an owner brings you a bird at 6:00 P.M. and then picks it up again at 8:00 A.M. a week later, do you charge for those two partial days? Do you merge the two partial days and call it one full day? To remove all doubt in this area a day is the day it arrives and another day is the day it leaves. Both days are counted. If an owner uses the times in the preceding example and has five boarding days in between, then the length of the visit was seven days, not six or five—seven. After all, you clean the cage when the owner is going to pick it up, and you have to add water and position it for the night regardless of when the bird was delivered. Every day counts when charging for boarding. This is common practice with kennels and veterinarians too.

When deciding if you should board birds, one great factor to take into consideration is noise. All birds make noise, some are just noisier than others. Generally speaking, the larger the bird the louder the bird can become. Parrots, which are generally quiet during the day, like to screech in the early morning when awakening and again just before bedtime. The noise a blue and gold macaw can make in one scream can be earsplitting! If you live near fussy neighbors, you'd better think twice before taking in a large bird which can make really loud and prolonged noises.

A good way to avoid having to vacuum around the cage(s) every single day is to use an old sheet over a table. I place the sheet over the table and drape it out as far as it will extend. Then I place the cage in the center of the table. This way the sheet catches the seed that spills near the table and cleaning up is easier.

Boarding Your Bird

We board very few birds. We limit our bird boarding because each guest in our home is treated as just that—a guest. The birds are incorporated into our daily family life and there may be as many as twenty distinct steps that we go through each day to make certain your bird is kept healthy, stimulated, active, and happy. These are:

- Uncover the cage each morning (6:00 A.M.).
- Morning talking and playing time.
- Change bottom liner of cage.
* Wash side liners.
- Clean surrounding area.
- Clean seed dishes and re-fill.
- Clean treat dishes and re-fill.
- Check gravel and re-fill.
* Prepare a bathing dish.
- Clean water dishes and re-fill.
* Add medication to water or seed.
* Dry cage from bath.
* Prepare fresh fruit.
* Prepare special treats.
* Clean perches.
- Replace all dishes and bottom liners.
- Afternoon talking and playing time.
- Check condition of feathers.
- Evening talking and playing time.
- Cover cage for bedtime (9:00 P.M.).

* if applicable

We charge $5.50 per day (or any portion thereof) per cage. Your bird will come home with only two additional qualities—*pampered and spoiled!*

_____ *Your pet deserves the best.* _____

Roger had his toy routine down pat,
He branded toys "his" by squashing them flat.

11 Keeping Your Ducks in a Row

This section of the book is dedicated to those things that most people absolutely hate—numbers. When you used to work for someone else you heard about forecasting, accounts receivable, accounts payable, expenses, debits, credits, and ledgers. You may not have been involved directly, but you probably didn't consider that side of the business too important to your paycheck or welfare. Now the shoe is literally on the other foot and you must consider that keeping numbers accurately, legibly, and neatly written in some logical sequence is mandatory for the health of your business.

Your accountant, your local tax office, and the Internal Revenue Service are not going to appreciate estimates and guesswork when it comes as a substitute for receipts and records. You must have proof of your transactions. There is no substitute for a simple record of those transactions. Here, then, is a simple, step-by-step method for keeping records. I hasten to add that this is a basic, suggested method for tracking your business. You may certainly wish to get into double-entry bookkeeping, or you could hire an accounting firm to handle all your transactions. This method is for those intrepid souls who like to keep an arms length from numbers and want the quickest method possible to avoid the misery of reconstructing figures from memory.

It is a safe generalization to say that two rules are mandatory:

Keep a copy of everything you purchase for the business by way of receipt.

Keep a record of everything you take in as income from any source whatsoever.

Even if you follow these two rules religiously, there are going to be areas where you forget to itemize expenses and write down income.

For years before I got into the pet sitting business I had an outside sales force. Each of my salespeople, regardless of the company into which I hired them, had expense accounts for which they were reimbursed. I would preface the introduction regarding expenses to each new salesperson with this declaration, "I know for a fact that you are cheating on your expense account." When hot denials from around the room subsided, I would add the following, "You are not cheating the company, you are cheating yourself by not claiming all your allowable expenses." This was true, without exception, for every salesperson.

Pay telephones, parking meters, tips on luncheon bills, coffee breaks, tips at car washes, and doughnuts for the office were only a few of the areas in which these people cheated themselves out of reimbursement by not claiming the items on the expense account form. True, it was only nickels and dimes for each expense, but the nickels and dimes add up quickly to dollars, and that is money never recovered!

You are in a business where you cannot afford to have expenses that are not listed. You cannot afford the luxury of forgetting a business lunch or a car wash. You need every legitimate deduction you can muster to keep your small business afloat.

I know full well that this portion of the book will not be a fun read for most of you. Please do not skip lightly over these pages though because everything you forget in your business costs is money you lose right off the top of your profits!

This section is not designed to be an aid to income tax preparation. It is designed only to teach you how to keep sufficient records to allow you the luxury of preparing your own income taxes, or of turning the records over to a professional who can do the itemization with correct and complete information.

I will not lie to you here and say that I kept every single scrap of paper as I should have right from the first day of my business life. I was remiss in my books and had to spend some time reconstructing expenses. It is far easier, I have learned, to do things properly the first time than to spend twice as long attempting to rectify mistakes. I have made myself a pledge to not let a full week pass without doing some of my paperwork so that the numbers will never again get out of hand. You should do likewise.

Recording Expenses

From the first day of your new business life you have expenses. You have paid money for some things. You have brought home those receipts from restaurants, gas stations, stationery stores and printers, and stacked them all in a pile on your desk. What are you going to do with all those receipts to keep them permanently filed in some logical order? You realize that for tax purposes you will have to keep those receipts for as many as seven years. There must be a logical approach to saving all this paperwork. You need an easy, fast, understandable method to not only log the information currently, but to retrieve it in the future should it become necessary as proof of purchase.

My method of recording expenses is so simple it only involves the following:

twelve blank sheets of paper
twelve legal envelopes
four file folders (third cut)
plastic tape.

Once you gather these four sets of things, you now have in front of you your entire year's worth of documents for recording all expenses incurred in your business. You also have permanent files for holding all this information for storage. Here's how you begin to utilize the papers.

Place one of these labels on each of the four file folders:

Expenses—First Quarter
Expenses—Second Quarter
Expenses—Third Quarter
Expenses—Fourth Quarter.

Three empty envelopes go into each file folder. On the first envelope write in the center *Expenses—January 199_* . On the second envelope write *Expenses—February 199_* . On the third envelope write *Expenses—March 199_* . These three envelopes go into the *Expenses—First Quarter* file folder.

Use the same procedure with the remaining nine envelopes by putting three months into each of the proper quarter's file folder.

Your twelve sheets of blank paper could be replaced by graph paper if writing in a straight line is not your forte. Graph paper makes the sheet easy to use. The first sheet is labelled at the top *Expenses—199_*. Down two spaces (on graph paper) and to the extreme left-hand side, you write January and underline it. Just two lines below that you run these headings across the page, from left to right: Date, Receipt #, Description, Cost, and Subtotals. You gather your weekly receipts in hand and sort them by date, beginning with the oldest date first. If you had an expense on the second of January, that would be the first one to itemize. If it were a receipt for auto maintenance, you put the date under the date column and number that receipt (somewhere on the face of it) with the number one and circle the number. Write the description under the description column, list the cost, and put the receipt into the envelope marked *Expenses—January 199_*.

As the sample sheet at the end of this chapter shows, you have twenty-six expense items for January. Each item is described by a proper category heading. The running subtotals are so you don't have to re-add the entire column at the end of the month. You can spot-check during the month to see how much you are spending compared with what you planned to spend.

When your month is completed, and all receipts for expenses during that month are gathered and logged on the sheet, you run a tape total. That tape total figure is your monthly expenses for January. You can write the total dollar figure on the outside of the receipt envelope, and then seal the envelope and tape it around the edges. Unless you are very unlucky, you will not have to open this envelope again. Just file it away for storage.

The numbering system only serves to help find the receipt again if you are forced to dig backwards through any given month. You may have some months where you have more than thirty receipts and must use a second page. The second page then becomes a continuation of that same month. You can keep three month's worth of receipts in one file folder. Keep the current quarter's folder in your active file and the rest in storage. File all four folders away when the year is done. This is a very basic method. Add all known costs for which you may have no receipts, too. Leave the receipt column blank and fill in all the known information.

Use your checkbook register as a cross-checking method of spotting all expenses. I commonly find that there are items for which I have written checks but have no receipts whatsoever. I add these to the monthly expense sheet also.

Another method of assuring yourself of getting receipts is to use credit cards and checks for purchases. Gas receipts are easy to forget unless purchased on a gasoline credit card.

A listing of common expense categories follows the sample expense sheet. You can use it as a reminder of expenses common to your business.

Expenses 199_

<u>January</u>

Date	Receipt #	Description	Cost	Subtotals
1/2	1	Auto Maintenance	$34.74	
1/2	2	Bond Renewal	122.29	
1/3	3	Gas	7.11	$164.14
1/5	4	Car Wash	6.95	
1/6	5	Doughnuts	32.45	
1/6	6	Gas	6.73	
1/9	7	Entertainment	30.98	
1/10	8	Gas	6.50	247.75
1/10	9	Postage	1.50	
1/11	10	Grief (sympathy) card	2.66	
1/13	11	Postage	1.05	
1/16	12	Postage	3.05	
1/17	13	Doughnuts	5.05	
1/17	14	Gas	7.65	
1/18	15	Postage	50.00	318.71
1/20	16	Car Wash	6.95	
1/20	17	Postage	1.45	
1/20	18	Gas	4.83	
1/21	19	Doughnuts	2.10	
1/22	20	Gas	6.96	
1/22	21	Flowers (bereavement)	21.00	
1/25	22	Gas	5.60	367.60
1/29	23	Gas	5.88	
1/29	24	Doughnuts	23.05	
1/29	25	Postage	.85	
1/20	26	Office Supplies	8.69	

Total January Expenses: $406.07

Expense Categories

Category	Includes
Advertising	Directories, newspaper ads, yellow pages, magazines
Auto Gas	Gas, oil, additives
Auto Maintenance	Any repairs to your work vehicle(s)
Auto Wash	Getting the car washed/waxed, weekly/monthly, including tipping
Bond	Bond cost, renewal
Bags	Plastic, for pickup of excrement, includes paper towels
Bank Charges	Account costs, service fees, check printing, checkbook, bad check charges
Business Cards	All purchased throughout the year
Business License	License in your city, or any other cities
Business Stationery	Any printed form which is repeated throughout the year with letterhead on it
Charity Donations	Work done, money given, or time devoted
Christmas Cards	Includes cards, stickers, gifts, etc.
Doughnuts	Monthly cost of purchase and distribution
Dues & Subscriptions	Associations, magazines, fees, memberships
Employment Costs	Advertising for help, forms, interview material
Entertainment	Legitimate expenses connected with the business
Flea Spray	Purchased for use in work, home servicing of your house, cost of purchase(s)
Magnets	Actual costs

Miscellaneous	Anything not covered on this list, by heading
Newsletter	Cost of printing, material, mailing
Office Rent	Portion of your house rent/mortgage which covers your office and garage for company car
Office Supplies	Pens, paper, pencils, calendars, usual office things
Permits & Special Licenses	Driving vehicle permits, area pass costs, city tax costs
Postage	Stamps, UPS, Federal, FAX, packages, mailing anything
Printing	Any printed material, photocopies, excluding stationery
Telephone	All costs for the telephone including answering machine
Utilities	Gas, water, lights, oil, air conditioning, office percentage
Work Clothing	Shirts, pants, shoes, rain gear, jackets, coats, sweaters

*Lulu was an only child who acted truly caring,
Placing food in front of each toy was her way of sharing.*

12 Accounts Receivable

Pet sitting for one customer, one time, is an easy task. You take back the key and collect your money with no problems. There are two types of customer for whom you do not have this clear-cut situation. First, there is the customer who calls you after arriving home and tells you to keep the key because that customer is going to use your service again. You are elated at the opportunity but—what about your check? You have to ask the customer to mail it. Second, there is your year-round repeat customer, for whom you always keep the key. Here, too, you have no reason to return to the home except to collect the check. That wastes your time; but, presuming this is a good customer, you would just as soon get the check in the mail anyway.

As long as these two types of customers mail their checks just as they said they would, you should never have any problems. But how do you know for certain you received the checks? Did that one pay in full? Was that the correct amount? Did I collect everything this month that I was owed? There is a way to make this easy for you and your customer.

First, I suggest you take out a post office box for all correspondence related to the business. A post office box is more professional than your home address and for many reasons you won't want everyone to know your home address when it is business-related. All correspondence relative to your business should go through this post office box. That includes checks.

To make it easy for a customer to send me a check, I leave a self-addressed envelope along with the statement for services after every sitting. To make the return envelope fit snugly into the package that I leave for the customer, I use an envelope which is slightly smaller than a regular legal-sized envelope so that one fits inside the other. To further distinguish payments from other correspondence, I use a different color for payment envelopes. The smaller-sized envelope doesn't cost any more than legal size to print and I don't have to pay more for the different color either. Your budget determines the printing quantity. I found that one thousand was an economical breaking point for ordering envelopes. If you consider the fact that your legal-sized envelope is used for all sorts of correspondence, including letters to the customers about their pets, you will probably use the entire one thousand envelopes in about a year.

A total of one thousand return envelopes for checks would be too much to hope for in one year, so I used many of the return envelopes for mailing out *Paw's Penny Post* on a quarterly basis. I re-ordered one thousand of both sizes of envelopes in about one year. Leaving a self-addressed return envelope is a good method of assuring prompt payment of your fee.

There is a very simple form of accounts receivable journal that you can maintain which will eliminate confusion when receiving customer checks. Go to the stationery store and buy a ruled accountant's tablet which has six numbered columns on the page. It is sometimes called an analysis pad. It is the size of typing paper and usually has fifty sheets to the pad.

Set up the six headings across the page just like the example at the end of the chapter.

If you keep all your customer records, files, and accounts receivable by the customer's last name, you will avoid confusion. The "follow date" is an arbitrary time (about two weeks) from the date you left the bill that you would telephone the customer and ask where the payment had been mailed. Fortunately, this won't occur too often. At this writing, we have never yet had a customer not pay us what was owed on the statement for services. Most people are very good about paying for pet care. If you do notice that some customer has been slow in paying for service, you might on any subsequent sitting require either a check prior to the sitting or at least payment of half of the total estimated fee. Any late payment demands some explanation. Your judgment prevails as to which customers warrant credit.

List the customer's last name in this (ie accounts receivable) journal and prepare the statement at the time you leave on the final sitting day. If you faithfully enter each billing, it will erase all doubt as to who has paid you and who has not.

At the end of each year you have from twelve to twenty-four sheets of paper reflecting twelve months' worth of income. It is all in one concise format. You can easily reconcile these monthly pages with your bank deposits for verification if you suspect you forgot to record either a deposit or a billing. The most common mistake I make is forgetting to record payments made by customers who leave me cash at the start of a sitting. Even for customers who leave you cash or a check at the start of a sitting, always prepare for them a statement for services marked paid and leave it at their home after the final sitting day.

126 Accounts Receivable

January Accounts Receivable

Bill Date	Customer Name	Amount Due	Follow Date	Date Rec'd	Running Subtotals	Amount Rec'd	Balance Due
1/2	Cotrich	$44.00		1/2		$50.00	+$6.00
1/2	Spellman	18.00		1/7		18.00	0
1/3	Smith, R.	93.00		1/4		93.00	0
1/4	Terry	18.00		1/7		18.00	0
1/4	Park	35.00		2/7*		35.00	0
1/4	Duncan	80.50		1/10		80.50	0
1/4	Trifle	36.00		1/12		36.00	0
1/5	Stoler	120.00		1/11		120.00	0
1/5	Altriemont	115.00		1/12		115.00	0
1/8	Zelinski	63.00		1/11		63.00	0
1/8	Smith, T.	13.00		1/8	$635.50	13.00	0
1/10	Samuels	224.00		1/13		224.00	0
1/11	Muggins	52.00		2/4*		52.00	0
1/11	Sheen	9.00		1/13		9.00	0
1/11	Sauterman	143.00		1/13	$1,063.50	144.39	+$1.39
1/15	Normans	27.00		1/17		27.00	0
1/15	Trundle	31.00		1/17		31.00	0
1/16	Smith, R.	13.00		1/17		13.00	0
1/16	Summers	45.00		1/21		45.00	0
1/16	Altriemont	31.00		1/21		31.00	0
1/16	Fugita	253.14		1/17		253.14	0
1/22	Morrison	27.00		2/3		36.00	0
1/22	Fugita	45.00		2/1		45.00	0
1/23	Trifle	45.00		2/1		45.00	0
1/24	Straun	35.00		1/25		35.00	0
1/25	Jackie	34.00		2/10		34.00	0
1/27	Doormer	90.00		2/10		90.00	0
1/29	Zelinski	27.00		2/3		27.00	0
1/29	Rubenstein	600.00		1/29		600.00	0
1/30	Straun	35.00		1/20		35.00	0
1/30	Liberos	48.00		2/8		48.00	0
1/31	Altriemont	69.00		2/8		69.00	0

Thirty-three Customers For A Total Of: $2,527.64

* payment was overdue, check customer's next sitting
+ $6.00 was a tip for good service
+ $1.39 was money expended on cat food
NOTE: Follow Date column is blank. List any date you had to call customer to ask for the check.

When it was time to change the litterbox, Pasha came on the run,
One quick squat was mandatory, that made the job great fun.

13 Was Your Year End a Success?

One year has been completed. You are now replete with records of expenses by month, sales by month, and receipts. These are all neatly tucked away into folders and your monthly envelopes are sealed. Now comes the time to make up an income/expense statement to see just how well you did during the past year. I did not call this a financial statement, nor a balance sheet. It is not that intense or complicated. This form is a statement of gross income and total expenses. Subtracting expenses from total income gives you your net profit for the year.

I take stock of my financial position on a monthly basis. You can do the same by starting a statement very first month you are in business.

This is not an accounting profile of your total income by any means. Many factors enter into your true financial picture. Some of these factors are:

> *spouse's income*
> *other business interests*
> *property sales*
> *tax credits and returns*
> *insurance losses*
> *medical payments/credits.*

Here we are only discussing your sitting business and whether it made enough money in this past year to be called profitable. Profit is not the only measure of success. I know many entrepreneurs whose spouses are employed in totally different and lucrative fields. These entrepreneurs would consider the business successful if expenses were just equal to sales. In these cases, the fun of the job is the object, not income.

At the end of the chapter is listed the income and expenses for a hypothetical calendar year. There is a maxim which states, "All change is not growth, as all movement is not forward." This will apply to your business during the second or third year. At some point you are going to reach a plateau where you must decide to expand with full force to continue doubling sales, or pull in your horns and be content with a fixed level of income. No business stands still for long. Every entrepreneur hits a certain plateau, and every entrepreneur must decide for better or worse to grow or slow. It is never a business decision, it is a personal decision. That decision rests entirely in your hands. You alone determine your own fate and the fate of your company.

Each January, as you stare at the figures for the preceding year, you may ponder the question about what direction you want to take your company. Every person has a different level of contentment. Your level of contentment lies deep within your own heart.

Your Pet Sitting Service

(Calendar Year 199_)

MONTH	GROSS INCOME	EXPENSES
January	$2,000.00	$470.33
February	1,648.00	570.25
March	2,408.00	647.14
April	2,124.00	417.76
May	1,672.00	392.11
June	4,048.00	404.40
July	5,110.56	610.56
August	4,243.92	569.74
September	3,992.00	512.69
October	2,874.00	295.21
November	3,874.00	318.21
December	4,928.00	574.86
Twelve-Month Total:	$38,922.48	$5,783.26
Minus Expenses:	−5,783.26	
Net Profit Total:	$33,139.22	

Humans threw the ball for Spot, that was always so,
Spot took the ball to Ralphie, but he would never throw.

14 Insurance — Do You Need It?

There are two types of insurance you should consider. Liability insurance and disability insurance. To avoid confusion, let's review what your existing bond does and does not cover.

Your bond is not insurance, it is a bond. Regardless of the size of your bond, whether $2,500 or $25,000, your bond will only become payable as a result of your own dishonesty, when you are convicted and put into jail. If you are accused of stealing an expensive diamond ring, the compensation will only be paid by your bonding company after your guilt has been established and proved. What would happen if that same diamond ring were lying on a bathroom counter and you accidentally knocked it into the toilet and it went down the drain? Would your bond cover that accident? No. This is where liability insurance comes into play.

Webster's dictionary defines liability as, "The state or fact of being legally responsible or under obligation; the extent to which one is liable, as for a debt." There is the key word, "legally." If you break a lamp in a customer's home or lose a pet out of the yard (assuming no negligence on your part) or a pet dies while under your care, you may well be held legally accountable by the owner. It is wise, therefore, to protect yourself with insurance against such an unlikely event occurring.

Let's take an absolute worst-case scenario. (Thankfully, I have never heard a horror story even close to anything this bad.) You are on a sitting where the customer asks you to cook a special meal for the pet. You heat some food on a gas stove, and after serving the meal you get distracted and forget to turn off the burner. The house is locked and that lit burner starts a fire. The fire causes a half-million dollars in damage. Do you seriously believe that you can avoid litigation from the owner of the home? Even if the owner has fire insurance, you can be assured that the owner's insurance company is not going to pay the bill. The owner's insurance company is going to look to you for compensation in this matter. If you don't have insurance and the case comes to a court hearing, you will lose! Your entire business could be wiped out with this one momentary lapse of memory. Now think of liability insurance.

There are side benefits to a liability insurance policy as well. What if your office burns up in a fire at your home? Most homeowner's policies (and renter's policies, too, for that matter) exclude protection for doing business from your own home. This means that even though you may have a maximum replacement value on everything in your home, your insurance company may just exclude anything in your office because it is (and was) a business location. This means your desk, typewriter, computer, files, records, books, etc.; all have to be replaced at your own expense. Liability insurance covers your office in your home.

What if you board birds in your home? Does your present home insurance provide coverage in case a boarded pet dies while under your care? Most regular policies either don't cover this sort of loss or require that a specific rider be added to your present policy to cover such contingencies. It can be an expensive rider to purchase as an inclusion on your existing policy. This, too, can be included in your liability insurance package. The combined type of coverage you wish for your business should be a written policy for a million dollars (combined coverage). This means a maximum payout of one million dollars, per claim, per incident. The likelihood of utilizing all this coverage is remote, yet I believe it is a necessary business expense to protect yourself from potential bankruptcy at the hands of an unexpected event.

Now let's talk about disability insurance. This is a gray area in most entrepreneur's minds because of the relationship of those people who may be working for you in the future. Many pet sitting firms hire associates who are classified as independent contractors. This status may or may not apply to relatives, friends, or others you employ to assist you in your business. Your personal liability in this matter is worth the consideration.

Disability is another word for legal incapacity; being unable to do the job due to injury or accident. If a person in your employ has an accident which is job related and does not have insurance, the state may intervene and hold you responsible to pay for all medical bills for that individual's specific injury. That person, even if a relative, may have no control over the course of the legal action. Disability insurance is your only shield against the medical and legal bills that may ensue in such an instance.

When you seek liability insurance, disability insurance, or any business-related form of insurance for your small company, you may be surprised to find that your regular, family-insurance agent may not be able to help you write the policy. Pet sitting, until recent years, was such a relatively new concept that many insurance companies either didn't want to be bothered with policies to cover such things, or were just not equipped to write liability or disability insurance for this particular entrepreneurial business. The third and worst-case choice we found was with big name companies that would write the insurance but at astronomical rates. We have been quoted rates on disability and liability policies set anywhere from $1,500 to $2,000 and more, for each policy, per year! This is certainly cost prohibitive to a small business.

Fortunately there are a few companies and a few agents who are willing and eager to write policies for this sort of business. In fact, some of these firms have enough group members to allow the company to lower the premiums to affordable rates for beginners. For specific information, details, and a rate quote, I strongly suggest that you contact one of these firms near where you live:

Company Name:	Nationwide Insurance
	1018 Brookstown Avenue
	Winston-Salem, North Carolina 27101
	(919) 723-5201
Contact Person:	Frank Burchette
Plan Provider:	Nationwide Insurance
Summary:	Coverage includes the client's pet(s), business personal property, bonds and non-owned auto available, availability of plan varies form state to state. Canadian coverage available through Nationwide Insurance at a local level.
Company Name:	Home Loan & Investment Company
	P.O. Box 100
	Grand Junction, Colorado 81502
	(303) 243-6600
Contact Person:	Jamie Hamilton
Plan Provider:	Scottsdale/National Casualty Insurance Company
Summary:	Available in all 50 states, $500,000 liability limit, minimum annual premium is $300, $250 deductible for

Insurance—Do You Need It?

bodily injury/property damage, plan does provide liability coverage for injuries sustained by the pet due to the sitter's negligence. Simple to file and use, bond coverage as well.

Company Name: Amwest Surety Insurance Company
100 California Street
Suite #720
San Francisco, California 94111
(415) 362-4300

Contact Person: Peter D. Holley

Plan Provider: Amwest Surety Insurance Company

Summary: Is in the bonding business only and issues dishonesty bonds which cover theft by an employee of the bonded company. Claims on this bond are paid when there is an arrest and conviction of the theft. Issues bond for one-year and three-year terms in California and over 40 other states. Application pending for Canadian coverage as well.

Company Name: Goodenough Insurance, Inc.
1927 Fifth Avenue
Suite #100
San Diego, California 92101
800-875-7160
FAX - (619) 232-7614

Contact Person: Dottie Bartz

Plan Provider: Great American Insurance Company

Summary: $1 million liability limit, non-owned auto coverage, business related personal property, bonds available, reasonable rates, available in all 50 states, liability extends to the client's pets.

I strongly suggest you shop around, compare rates, and get the policy(ies) best suited for your specific needs. For example, a $10,000 bond is of no more value than a $1,000 bond unless you intend to collect by convicting yourself! The $10,000 bond only appears more impressive to a potential customer. Is it worth the extra dollars? You be the judge.

Certain dogs trade toys easily, others are very tough,
Queenie would trade anything, to get her ball was enough.

15 What's in a Name?

You have named your company and now find your company name gaining acceptance throughout your selling area. You enjoy the name of your firm. You take great pride in using the name you have created. Suddenly, without any warning, a legal-sized envelope arrives in the mail bearing the return address of a thirty-man law firm. The letter inside contains the grim order for you to cease and desist using your name because you are infringing on a service mark which has been registered by another company. Reading further on in the letter, you discover that the company name you are using to which this other business claims ownership is not even in your area. It is over a thousand miles away in another city. What legal rights do you have? Let's go back to the beginning.

The time to protect your company name is after the first six months you are in business. Once you find that you enjoy the name and decide that you will be using it in it's final form, then it is time to protect your good name. Why do I say wait six months? The name you start out using may well not be the name you end up keeping. I started Paw Partners by calling it Professional Executive Trust Services. I thought that would be cute because the first letters of each word spell out PETS. Not cute. It sounded too stuffy, formal, expensive, and legal. Paw Partners conveyed the message much more clearly. I didn't come up with the title Paw Partners until well into the third month of my new business. Had I decided to begin the legal process of trying to service mark the words "Professional Executive Trust Services," it would have been a waste of time, money, and effort.

That's why it's important to use your new name for six months to get a feel for it. See if people respond to the name. Some company names convey no message whatsoever. National-General Company, for example, leaves you with no visual picture of that company's business interest. You want to portray a visual picture of what you are going to do for the customer. Many small pet sitting firms simply put their name first and then what they do, such as "John Jones Pet Sitting Service." Not too creative, but it conveys the message. But what if another John Jones is busy making dog food and he's not your brother? Now we face the problem of copyright, trademark, service mark, and patent.

Each state has a department which handles trademarks. In California, for example, it is handled through the Secretary of

State's office. At present in California you submit a form (provided free by the state) along with three copies of the mark on which you wish exclusive rights of ownership. You include a fifty dollar ($50) filing fee, and you should get a response within ten to twelve weeks. What the state does is research the record books of all persons who have filed for such applications previously, and if that specific name has not been taken, you are then granted the rights. This means that in California, at least, you are protected against someone opening up a business in your town (or any town in the state) and calling it by the same name you have chosen. The reason for this person using your name could be accidental; but it could be intentional. A competitor's attempt to gain profit from your established good record.

You can file for a trademark or service mark in your own state as soon as you are certain the name you have chosen is the one you are going to use permanently. The likelihood of infringement on your company name is diminished by the complexity of the name. For example, if you name your business "John Jones Pet Sitting Service of Vancouver," it is extremely doubtful that anyone is going to accidentally copy that name. However, if you decide to name your business more generically, "Fur, Fins and Feathers," it is very likely that many people have not only thought about that name, but also someone may have filed long before you went into business.

If you live near your state capitol, you can save time on this filing procedure simply by going into the Hall of Records at the capitol and asking to see the book in which all trade names and service marks are filed. This information is open to the public so you could readily see if a name you wish to apply for is already taken. Think of it being like vanity plates on your car. When you order vanity plates, you cannot use a combination anyone else has already used. When you go into the Department of Motor Vehicles, the clerk looks in a book (or on the computer) to see if that specific name is already used. If so, you can't have it. The same is true with trademarks and service marks.

Once your application is processed by the state in which you live, your service mark is protected for a period of seven years without renewal. At the end of that seven-year period, you must renew the application to keep it effective.

Unless you plan to expand your business operation to another state, or you have picked a very generic name for your firm, filing within your state is usually enough. If you do plan to expand your operation into surrounding areas, you should know that a federal copyright, patent, trademark, or service mark takes precedent over state's rights. This means that just because you have filed in Oregon, you cannot automatically use the name in Washington without worry of infringement. Coupled with that fact, if someone has filed for a federal service mark, it takes precedent over all state's rights. You could still lose your name if someone has filed federally and decides they don't want you using part of their name!

This problem of naming a business has become even more critical with the recent explosion of franchising. Pet sitting itself is now becoming a franchise business in many areas. People just like yourself pay up to $10,000 to get a new business started. Along with this new business comes a new name which is also given to you. Franchiser's protect that name dearly. You can't use protected names. Appearing in court to protest will do no good. People who file federally have the protection of the court.

The ultimate safety comes in filing with the federal government in Washington, D.C. At present, this filing costs $175 and you can receive a free booklet with all the necessary information you need by contacting:

United States Patent and Trademark Office
Public Service Center
CP4-1A01
Washington, D.C. 20231
(703) 557-4636

If you want further general information about copyrights from the federal government, you can telephone (202) 479-0700.

You may have seen advertisements in some business magazines in which firms advertise to research available names for your business. You can do this same work yourself—for nothing! If you join the National Association of Pet Sitters, you receive a listing of all pet sitting firms in the United States which belong to the association. There are over 300 names in that directory which are already taken for the pet sitting business. It is a good place to start your research for a permanent name. (More about the National Association of Pet Sitters in a later chapter.)

There are legal firms which will do the research, guidance, counseling, and forms for you, but be prepared for an expensive bill. A current fee range is from $250 to $500. Save your money and deal with the government directly. It is good experience to learn how the system of bureaucracy works.

Finally, a personal aside on the question of business names. I feel that the use of the word animal in a name is inappropriate. You don't sit with animals—you sit with pets. Animals belong in a zoo. Pets belong in a home!

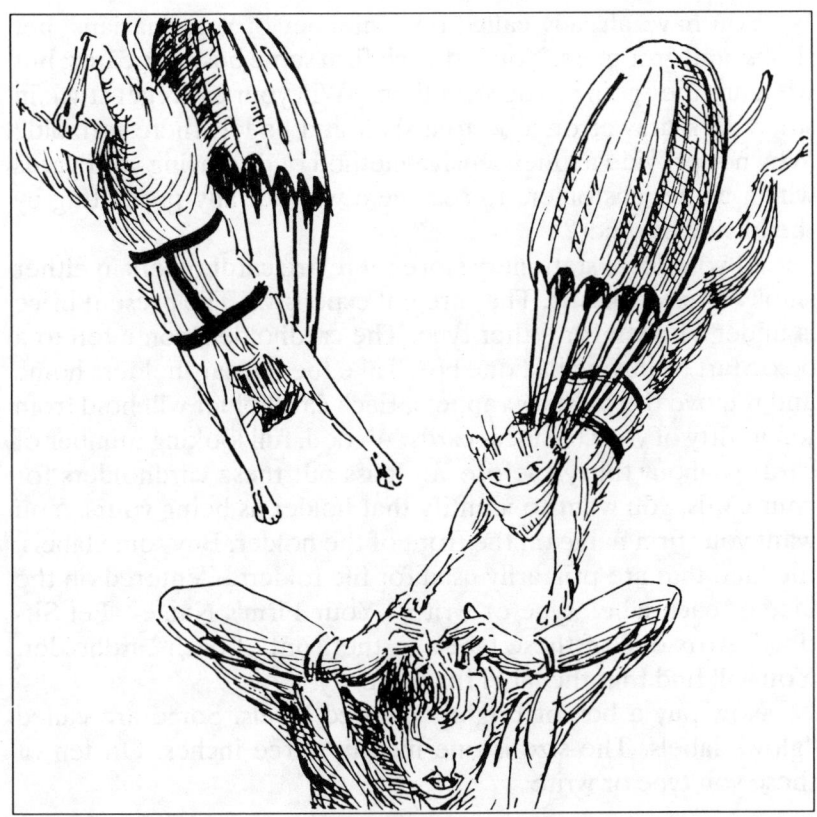

When you walk into a house, you may hesitate or hedge,
But you never expect cats to be up high on a ledge.
Hewey and Louie had a game they adore—
Jump on your back and knock you to the floor!

16 Cardholders and Doughnuts

Cardholders and doughnuts do have something in common. You will see the doughnut connection in a moment. First the cardholders.

You have already called on a number of veterinarians, pet shops, and groomers. You left each firm some business cards; but what are they going to do with them? Will your cards get stuck in some dark drawer on a bottom shelf and be left there to mold? Why not provide an inexpensive method of displaying your cards which allows customers to see them without any prompting by the business owner?

At your local stationery store there are cardholders in either smoky or clear plastic. They are not expensive. The present price is under $1 each for either type. The cardholders come ten to a box. Start by buying just one box. Take the ten cardholders home and remove the plastic wrappers. Each cardholder will hold from ten to fifty of your business cards. A good, full looking number of cards is about thirty. Before you pass out these cardholders for your cards, you want to identify that holder as being yours. You want your firm name on the front of the holder. Buy some labels, the kind that are primarily used for file folders. Centered on the face of each label, type or write, "Your Firm's Name—Pet Sitting." Affix one of these labels to the front of each cardholder. You will find that the label fits perfectly.

Now buy a box of brightly colored labels. Some are called "glow" labels. The size is one inch by three inches. On ten of these you type or write:

> *If this cardholder is empty, please call: (213) 555-1212 for prompt refill! Thank you very much. (Name of firm here.)*

Stick one of these to the inside back of each cardholder. Now you are ready to fill each cardholder with business cards.

The reason for the stickers on the cardholder is twofold:

> It identifies the holder as being yours. Many cardholders look alike. If you return to the store two weeks later and find someone else's cards in your holder, how do you prove the cardholder is yours?
>
> It gives you a gauge as to how fast your cards move in that location. Many store owners call me routinely to tell

me they are out of cards, even though I was just there a week before!

Armed with your new cardholders, you return to every veterinarian, pet shop, and groomer you have visited previously and ask them if they would like to have a cardholder to display your cards. The key word here is *display*. Anybody can take a free cardholder, but if it's going to sit under the counter or behind the brine shrimp, it won't do any selling for you. You want to be assured that this individual is going to let you display your cards in a prominent position. Being positioned right next to the cash register is ideal. At one time or another, every customer ends up next to the till. However, any point of prominence will do.

You will find that about half of all the stores you visit will let you display your cards. Groomers are the most willing, pet shops are next, but veterinarians are sometimes reluctant to exhibit what they consider promotional material for other products. Probably only 10 percent of all vets you visit will allow you to display your cards.

Assure each person you visit that if they display your cards you will come by, on a regular basis, and make certain that the container is kept full. This is a good trade-off for free advertising. When you have finished your route, type up a list of the firms where you placed cardholders. This list can be used as a master check list to remind and assure yourself that you have "made the rounds" to every store you promised to service with your cards.

Every firm that maintains a cardholder for you should be put on your doughnut run. Why doughnuts? Because *everybody* eats doughnuts. People on a diet won't eat candy. Liquor is too controversial. Fresh fruit is nice, but seasonal and expensive. We tried many ideas as a reward for referrals, but stayed with doughnuts because doughnuts were so popular with the people in these businesses.

Most people who call upon veterinarians, pet shops, and groomers are trying to sell that business something. You are one of only a few who is going to come in on a regular basis and give them something for nothing! You should try to schedule a doughnut run at least once a month. I regularly call upon thirty-eight different businesses which refer people to my service. I spread this delivery over three mornings so that all the doughnuts get delivered to the businesses prior to noon. I have yet to find a person who doesn't appreciate doughnuts in the morning.

Think of your cardholders as the "lifeblood" of your business. You must keep your name in front of the public and there is no better method than having free advertising sitting on counters where the public shops. This will be the primary source of your referral business until neighbors and friends of past customers recommend you to others.

I don't want to leave you with the impression that this is the only effective form of advertising. I also want you to know that I have tried many, many, other forms of advertising to attract customers. Direct mailings, mass mailings, newspapers, church bulletins, dog shows, handouts, and contests are all methods that I have tried for adding new customers. Nothing yet has been nearly as effective as the referrals from related businesses. Regardless of what new source of advertising I tried, for every new customer I got from that new source, I still got ten from the cardholders.

The more often you visit with veterinarians, pet shops, and groomers, the more business you will get. The more familiar you become with the business owners, the more calls to come to your telephone from interested prospects.

Left me alone? Rover said, "I'm really mad."
He hid in the woods, feeling lonely and sad.
Six hours of searching, from place to place,
The owners found Rover and got a lick in the face.

17 Why Have all the Answers?

From your first day in business you are going to be swamped with telephone calls and questions for which you have no answers.

Do you know anybody who boards cats?
Do you know anybody who maintains office aquariums?
I have to board my dog, can you recommend a good kennel?
Do you know anybody who will stay in my home for a week?
Do you know anybody who clips birds' toes?
Do you know where I can buy dog and cat presents?
If you don't sit in my area—who does?

I like to think of any person asking questions as a potential customer or future referral. I just hate telling people that I really don't have any idea. To avoid being ignorant, the easiest way to get the information is to ask your own questions every time you visit a pet shop, groomer, or veterinarian. Take business cards of competitors, dog trainers, handlers, groomers, kennels, and maintenance people. As you get these names, compile them into a list and put it by your telephone for reference.

Every time you get a new question to which you have no answer, take that question along on your next doughnut run. The most recent question I asked of business owners on my doughnut run was, "Where can a person buy a Vietnamese potbellied pig?"

Customers are going to rely upon your judgment when it comes to flea sprays, flea spray services, types of dog food, vitamins, brushes, combs, veterinarians, operations, and even laxatives! Referring people to the right source for getting what they want always pays great dividends in the long run. You will have the favors returned to you in a myriad of ways.

In addition to veterinarians, pet shops, groomers, and trainers, there is another excellent source for specific information about pets. This comes from joining associations which specialize in your business—pet sitting. There may be local organizations in your area which have meetings you can attend. If there is no local organization, there is the national organization.

The National Association of Pet Sitters will allow you to apply for membership after you are fully involved in the business of pet sitting.

At present, the annual membership dues are very modest and you may write for information to the following:

Ms. Patti J. Moran, Executive Director
National Association of Pet Sitters
632 Holly Avenue
Winston-Salem, North Carolina 27101.

As a member of the National Association of Pet Sitters you will be part of a campaign promoting the concept of pet sitting and high ethical business standards.

The National Association of Pet Sitters is a nonprofit organization which will keep you abreast of the latest trends and movements in our industry. I must admit I am biased in favor of this organization since I am on the board of directors promoting membership.

If you want to get involved on a more intimate and personal basis with others in your same occupation, try telephoning competitors. It may sound odd, but if you talk with other pet sitters who work in areas adjacent to your own, you will find many areas of common interest. I meet regularly with two other firms and we never lack topics of conversation. At every meeting I learn something new about our business. An added bonus of these relationships is mutual referrals. I send many customers to them and they do likewise for me. We know each other, trust each other, and respect each other's work.

In your area there should be at least one veterinarian who specializes in certain types of pets. You need to get to know these veterinarians, as well as pet shops which specialize, so you can refer people who inquire about each of the following types of pets: dogs, cats, birds, tropical fish, saltwater fish, goldfish, hamsters, horses, rabbits, turtles, snakes, exotic animals

The more people you are able to refer to good sources of reference, the more valuable you become in the eyes of your customers.

Prissy liked to run even faster than a bike,
But just try to tow her and she sat down on strike!

18 A Formal Presentation Book

Once you have been in business for five or six months, you will find that you have accumulated a great number of things that should be organized and shown to prospective customers during the initial interview. Things like unsolicited letters of appreciation for your good work, business cards for noncompetitive companies, a copy of your surety bond, your insurance policy, your customer list, pet pictures, etc. All these items can and should be organized into one neat, tidy, professional-looking presentation book.

My particular presentation book is seventeen pages long and bound in a three-ring format. When the interview forms and literature are fitted into the front pocket of the book and a calendar and return envelope (for mailing a key if the customer doesn't have a spare) are tucked into the rear pocket of the book, I then have everything I need to take into a prospective customer's home for that first interview. Everything in that book is arranged in the order I would like the customer to view it. I use a black three-ring binder with small rings. The entire notebook is only 9½ by 11½ inches in size. Each page has a sheet front and back and, to make certain nothing gets soiled, I have each page inside a glassine sheet.

The following is a description, from front to back, of what is on each page in my book. Your book should be in the order best suited to your own personal taste.

Business License and Insurance

On the very first page I have my city business license and a card each from my insurance agent and my bonding agency. This is to reassure the client that I am a respectable member of the community. You can also have, for example, a copy of your membership in the Better Business Bureau, if you choose.

On the next page (backside) I have my certificate of membership in the National Association of Pet Sitters. This usually elicits the comment from each prospect, "Oh, I didn't know there was such a thing as an association as Pet Sitters!"

On the next page, front and back, is the full copy of my surety bond so the customer can be assured that I am bonded. On the next page is the code of ethics for the National Association of Pet

Sitters. Following that is a list of fifteen items put out by the same association called, "What to look for in a Reputable Pet Sitter."

I go through each page slowly, explaining what each item is and why it is important to the customer. You explain it because the item is there for the customer's benefit—not yours. Anytime a customer has questions, I stop the presentation and answer the question fully.

References

The next eight pages are devoted to references. The first pages of this section contain lists with the headings Sitting References. Here you list your latest (or all) sitting jobs. Don't keep the list in alphabetical order, just add to the list as new customers come along. I simply show the customer's name, city, and telephone number. I use a highlighter pen to denote each customer name which is a repeat customer. At the bottom of the page I put the note, "highlighted names denote repeat customers, some on a year-round basis."

After sitting references comes a page headed Pet Shop and Grooming References. Here, again, you simply add the name of any pet shop or groomer who has referred a customer to you in the past months. The next page is Veterinarian References. Same as the previous pages, add names as they come to you from referrals. The last page of references is for Kennel References. You will find that within six months it will be no effort at all to have fifty or more names listed in your referral section.

Miscellaneous

On the very next page I have centered a picture of my three poodles surrounded by six business cards of noncompetitive businesses. Most customers ooh and aah over the doggies and I explain that the business cards belong to firms that I recommend. Some of the business cards that I have shown are:

a pet door manufacturer
a great place to buy birds
a party supply company for pet gifts
an aquarium maintenance company
a good gardening firm
a good kennel.

The next page has business cards with more information. You may wish to include groomers, pet shops, feed stores, etc.

The last two pages of the presentation book display unsolicited letters of appreciation from customers. Handwritten notes of sincere thanks that we receive regularly for doing a good job. Handwritten notes are much more appealing than a formal, blocked, typewritten letter on company stationery. You can solicit customers to send you these letters if you wish, but I think you will find that if you are doing a good job, the customers will just send them to you automatically. Some of the best notes of thanks have been written to us on the back of the statement for services and returned to us with the check! Here is an actual example of one note which can really make you feel your job is worthwhile:

Dear Bill & Ellen,

    Thank you so much for caring for our schnauzer Paulie. She was so happy and content when we came home. We know she was loved, played with, and cared for just as we would. We'd like you to keep the keys so that when we go again we'll be all set.

    Thanks again,

Sheri Taylor

You will find yourself saving all these notes religiously because they are valuable reminders of what a great service you perform for your customers!

Your presentation book should be adaptable. You may feel after a certain point in your career that you only want to list repeat customers for reference. That's fine. You may want ten or twelve pages of unsolicited letters of appreciation. Your presentation book should be arranged to complement your presentation, not hinder it. Any arrangement which allows your presentation to move more smoothly is beneficial.

*Old Smoke was a hunter who did his duties gladly,
This was his fourth skunk—a present for Daddy.*

19 Odds and Ends

In any business there are small details that don't fit neatly into your daily plans. Here, too, I have put those small, but important, odds and ends.

Establishing a Routine

Once you have gotten the "bugs" out of your working system and have most of your chores down pat, it is time to work out a routine that suits your weekly and monthly needs. I cannot recommend exactly what to do on any specific day because your week is going to be governed by the number of sitting assignments you have and the amount of free time between your jobs. You will find that you need to establish frequent calls on pet shops, veterinarians, groomers, etc., to keep your cardholders full. Further, you have to cover those businesses who didn't wish to display your cards, but were nice enough to accept them and hand them out to anybody who asked.

Let me give you an example of my situation and you can adapt yours accordingly:

Number of businesses carrying my cardholders is 39
Number of businesses without cardholders which should be called upon regularly anyway is 22
Number of businesses to call upon weekly is 15
Monthly average of businesses which get doughnuts is 44.

You can see from these numbers that I must allow in my weekly routine for three half-days to stock cards in cardholders, deliver doughnuts, and visit with merchants.

If you are working at pet sitting full time, you will find, mercifully, that there is a lull during midday that allows you to get these routine chores done. Repeat customers and customers with young dogs and cats usually need twice-a-day visits. These must be spaced well apart. You will find your heaviest clientele are booked in the early morning and the early evening. These are the two busiest times of the day. In the interim you can usually find time to deliver your doughnuts, stock cards, and the like.

You also have to find time during that midday lull to catch up on paperwork such as:

preparing statements

typing (or writing) letters summarizing the sittings
typing (or writing) letters from telephone inquiries
preparing the daily check list sheets for the next day's work
routing your calls for the following day
preparing for evening interviews
keeping your three-by-five-inch merchant cards up to date
banking checks and balancing accounts receivable
itemizing expenses in your journal

This is not a lot of work as long as you don't let it get too far behind. If you get a couple of weeks behind in any one area (my weakness is entering expenses), then it becomes real drudgery!

One organizational tip that really helps in my routine is to utilize a blackboard for listing calls. Any day that I have more than seven sittings to perform, I haul out my board and start writing in names and times. I get them all organized on the board until it's clear in my mind how I am going to service these accounts in the proper order, at the appointed time, and with the least amount of driving. I then transfer the information into my appointment book and then follow my own good advice. This logical sequence can be planned out on a blackboard, whiteboard, or even three-by-five-inch cards arranged on a desk with customer names written on them. Any method which organizes your day better is a great help and time saver.

You may also find, as I have, that many of your regular customers prefer to be billed on a monthly basis. If you determine through a past month's history that a particular customer pays the bill regularly and you have no problems with collection, it will be easier for both you and the customer to start using a once-a-month statement. I have one customer who uses our service at least two days every week. It became foolish to leave a bill each time, receive a check, and then deposit the small checks into the bank each week. I now bill this customer once a month and deposit one large check each month.

You will need to develop your own form for the once-a-month statement. I use a form similar to the statement for services, but with itemized dates and times.

What about the Telephone?

There are a lot of differing theories about what makes good and what makes bad telephone etiquette. The main questions center around these five points:

> *Should you use an answering service instead of a machine?*
> *What should be on your recording or service?*
> *Do you call back everyone who calls?*
> *Do you follow up leads?*
> *What can you sell on the telephone?*

There are armed camps among pet sitters on either side of the question of whether an answering service is better than a machine. On the side of an answering service is the personalized touch of a human speaking to the prospect. Many people do not like speaking to a machine (recording) and would much rather talk with a real person. These same people may not leave any message and simply dial the next sitter on the list instead of waiting for a return call from the message left on the answering machine.

On the opposite side of the issue, opponents of live service cite the cost as a factor against, along with the question of information. What can a service really tell a caller about your business? Other than taking a name and telephone number, you really don't want your service quoting prices, answering technical questions, or nullifying a potential customer's interest with an improper answer. The only true service a live person can perform is to assure the caller that you will call that person very soon. A live person can clear up the slurred speech and can correctly record the indistinct telephone numbers which make recordings useless. Be aware, however, that I have used many answering services in my past affiliations where the reverse was also true! Tired operators suffered momentary lapses of memory and recorded wrong telephone numbers and incorrect names. Receiving an incorrect telephone number is the most frustrating thing in the world since retrieval is almost impossible.

The correct solution for you is measured by the pocketbook and by the amount of time you can devote to answering the telephone personally at home when it rings. We try to devote most Mondays, Tuesdays, and Wednesdays to telephone answering when possible. Those are the days when we get the bulk of our inquiries. The rest of the week the calls are fewer and more random. Calling prospects back within two hours is a good way to overcome the impersonal nature of using recording devices.

There is also a dichotomy of thought regarding what should be on a recording or service. Many pet sitters use long message tapes and attempt to sell themselves to the prospect by extolling the virtues of the company within the message itself. Some sitters simply ask the party to leave a name and address and say that further information will be mailed out. We favor another approach. We only give out the name of our company and say that we will return the call as soon as possible. All our messages are twenty seconds or less in length. We only ask for a name and telephone number.

You can lease or buy fantastic equipment from your telephone company which will allow the calling party to skip the message, if the party has heard the message before, by pressing the star sign on the phone to get right to the message-leaving section. You can also add equipment which allows callers to play one of nine messages as interests permit. (i.e. cats—press 7, dogs—press 8, birds—press 6, and so forth.)

I personally do not believe that people like to camp on the telephone listening to a canned sales pitch which goes on and on through a litany of services and rates. Many times you are going to get calls from a prospective customer which begin like this:

> *I have a rather special and unique situation which needs some explanation. You see, my dog Frosty is not really a pet, but a member of our family. He's our child, and I need someone who understands—*

Read the preceding statement six months from now and you will laugh out loud! You will, by then, have had at least *fifty* calls which began like this. This inquirer doesn't care what you normally do for other callers who press button number two. This caller wants *special* service! This is a special dog, requiring special care, and only you can talk intelligently to this person about their needs. I believe that messages extolling the virtues of routine service are a waste of time for this particular customer. You need to call this person back and talk about Frosty. Nothing else is a good substitute. Even if you had a live service handling that call, the operator is not going to have the proper answers to Frosty's needs. Only you have those answers.

One of the luxuries of expanding your business after your first year is to have someone, even if only part time, to answer the telephone and talk to callers about pet needs. Until you can afford that, a twenty-second message, changed frequently to prevent boredom, is certainly adequate.

Do you call back everyone who calls? Most emphatically—yes! I know many sitters who simply ignore calls which sound odd, unreasonable, or complex. We had a call recently on the recorder from a gentleman who had an arthritic ninety-pound German shepherd which had to be carried up and down a flight of stairs for bowel elimination twice a day. I knew that we could not help him with his needs but we called him back to recommend someone who could. It is not only common courtesy, but also good business practice to refer people to someone else who can help. Return all phone calls regardless of the strange nature of the request. In the long run, it will enhance your image as a professional in a world filled with amateurs.

Following up leads involves calling back individuals who have requested literature or mentioned calling you back at a later date. At present, we have enough business so that I have not been involved in calling back potential customers. It is, however, a good idea for slow business periods.

You can set up a tickler file dated thirty days from the date of the original call. When you receive an inquiry for which you mailed out literature, you file it thirty days from the date of the mailing. Every day you check to see who you should be calling for follow-up detail.

I don't consider this form of follow-up call solicitation because that caller originally called you for information. You are just following it up to see if there is anything further you can do for that person. Many people are uncomfortable with this form of follow-up. If you are one of those people who feel nervous and jittery about talking to someone who is not truly a warm prospect, then it is best not to call at all. but much gold can be mined through calls to people who just forgot about your service. Gentle telephone reminders can bring bookings!

This last question is very important. There are some pet sitters who absolutely refuse to interview someone unless that person commits to a booking over the phone. I think this practice is insulting to the customer. How many services or products do you buy over the telephone sight unseen? Not many, I would venture to guess. I buy nothing over the telephone. I want to meet that person, that company, or see that product involved before I commit to any decision which involves money. I cannot imagine why anyone would agree to a sitting without personally meeting the sitter or owner of the firm. All you can realistically sell over the telephone is the interview date. (The exception to this rule is a referral from a past customer, such as a next-door neighbor.)

My only objective in talking with any prospect is selling a time to visit that person and meet the pets. That's all, and nothing else. I only use the twenty-two item check list and the rest of our services as bait to entice the caller to invite me to the home. Even the telephone company will admit that no product can be totally sold over the telephone. The telephone is a tool to get interviews, not bookings.

Award Winners

After your first year in business, during which you were working full time at pet sitting, you will have seen from 150 to 250 pets. In our first year in business we saw just over 240 pets. From our own discussions about the differing and unique personalities of pets, we noted that we favored some pets more than others. We liked some cats, we disliked some dogs, we enjoyed some pairs of pets, and disliked entire families of pets! My wife and I started talking about the pets we truly enjoyed sitting with during the preceding twelve months and said to ourselves, "Why not create an award for the best?" We didn't know at that time for what category the best exactly referred to. We talked about letting all of our customers know who were the best dogs and cats. We immediately discarded that idea because it would make those customers who didn't win very unhappy. We arrived at a plan, and here's what you can do to make some of your customers happy and active repeat users of your service.

Think back over all the unique, different, unusual, or abnormal things pets did for and to you during the past year. For example, we had one dog who could actually sing! Bob was a schnauzer which you could hold in your arms while singing "Rock-a-bye Baby," and he would growl-howl along with you, all through the song. Another dog, Jamie, had a unique smile. This dog used the reflex reaction for anger (the bearing of teeth) as a sign for happiness and would flash a toothy smile ten to fifteen times during each visit. We created two special categories of awards to cover these two dogs—smiling and singing.

The range of award categories can be from one to as high as twenty, if you can think up enough titles that merit that many awards. Here is a suggested list from our first-year award winners:

Best all-around mannerly good dog
Best overall dogs (in one family)
Cutest cat
Cutest dog
Character award (unusual behavior)
Best lover (dog)
Best lover (cat)
Best singer
Best smiler
Most loving cat.

You can see that some of the categories (such as the first and second) are almost identical, but we had two candidates who deserved the award so we just added a separate category to accommodate both sets.

Next go to your local office supply or stationery store and find some blank award certificates. Even if you are not an artist, you can buy a wide calligraphy pen and some India ink and script the message onto the face of the scroll. Along with the award for dogs, we bought an oversized biscuit and wrapped it in gold foil. For cats, we purchased a catnip mouse and wrapped that in gold foil. We composed a letter to be presented to the "parents" of the lucky recipients of the awards. The letter is shown in it's entirety at the end of the chapter. With some minor modifications, you can duplicate this letter for your own use.

Whenever possible, you should present this award in person. The look on your customer's face upon being presented with the certificate, foil-wrapped gift, and letter is worth 1,000 words! The recipient is shocked! If you think all this sounds silly, think again. Our past winners have those certificates framed in expensive frames and centered on walls in dining rooms, living rooms, and dens. Anywhere that visitors can see and comment on the award it is displayed. People are proud of their pets, and people are thrilled at having the pet receive any sort of commendation.

Remember that these awards are only effective for the ten or so recipients that you select each year. It is of no value to publish or make public the winning list to any other prospect or customer. In fact, publishing the list can actually do damage because it points out all your other customers as losers. I suggest that you never tell other customers how many categories were in consideration. It is just a fun activity that promotes good will for the recipients and adds credibility to your firm. You will find that these awards, just like the doughnut runs to pet shops, groomers, and veterinarians, are the highlight of your work routine. Anytime you can brighten a customer's day with something new and novel, it is bound to be well received. Once you institute your own annual awards, you will be looking for unusual actions in pets you sit with as potential award winners for next year.

An Asset to the Community

If your only goal in the pet sitting business is making money, then you should be in another business. There are many, many fields which are much more lucrative, monetarily rewarding, and comfort oriented than the pet sitting business. After all, the bottom line to this business is picking up animal excrement. How exciting can that be?

Your true goal as a pet sitter is doing a job that matters and having fun while you are making money. I can think of no job in the world where I can set my own hours, establish my own procedures, work at my own pace, play and romp with pets that I love, and be paid to do it!

There are many things you can do to make your own firm the absolute best in your area. First and foremost is credibility. Doing what you say you will do, being on time, keeping your word, having a friendly attitude, and showing a real concern for the needs of the pets you serve; all of these characteristics and more will shine forth and build your credibility. Recommendations from allied companies (recommendations which hold over the years) do not come easily in this business if you don't provide good deeds which warrant praise. How often have you recommended a good restaurant only to have your friends say the meal was terrible? Did you recommend that restaurant again?

When you think about it, you are asking people to place under your care possibly the three most important possessions they have: their homes, their pets, and their automobiles. How many strangers would you trust with those three possessions?

There are many ways you can favor your customers which do not involve spending money out of your pocket. Here are a few.

Test Products

After you have been in business for five or six months, you can use the ads you see in trade magazines concerning new or revolutionary products for dog and cat care (or you might see a new product sitting on the shelf at your local pet store). Do not hesitate to call up the manufacturer, explain who you are and what you do, and ask for a free sample of the product to give to your customers to "test." (Never, ever, do any tests yourself; you will be biased one way or another.) If the test works and is favorable, tell the manufacturer you will use your newsletter to recommend the product to your customers and prospects.

Charities

Many customers donate to charities on a regular basis. Many of those same customers would like the charity to be pet-related but don't know the names or functions of pet charities. There are many charities which you can recommend to your customers, charities that desperately need assistance taking care of pets; everything from free spaying and neutering clinics to providing free pets for senior citizens.

You can contact all of these charities directly and ask for their newsletters, which will give you a good background on the services that the charities provide.

Legal Assistance

Some people might wish to provide for their dog(s) or cat(s) in the form of a will. Daily maintenance, for example, to keep the dog or cat fed and healthy for the rest of its natural life. Where do you find a good attorney who can draft a document so that the greedy relatives cannot declare aunt Gertrude senile and have the will overturned? There are attorneys who specialize in just such wills, and by checking with your local bar association, you can get a referral for two or three. You can talk with these individuals and then recommend one or more of them to customers.

Fund Raisers

Sometime within the first six months of your operation, somebody from a nonprofit organization is going to ask you for a donation to help their worthwhile cause. If you judge the cause truly worthwhile, why not donate time for sitting. A free sitting day is a valuable commodity to them, yet it does not cost you cash out-of-pocket to offer as a prize. (It is a real cost to you because your time is money.) Your bonus is getting free advertising in the bargain!

Suggestions

Some pet owners are extremely busy people and haven't the time or energy to think of ways to help their pets while they are away. Small suggestions, like portable radios playing where the pet can hear it or a larger water dish in the backyard, can be greatly appreciated by the customer.

Many ideas that seem obvious to you may not even have entered the mind of your customer. Take the time to leave suggestions in the letter you leave after your last sitting day. You will be amazed at how many people take your advice.

Nonprofit Involvement

In order to maintain credibility, it is vital that you have absolutely no monetary interest in any of the previously mentioned ideas, people, products, and suggestions. There will certainly be temptations. One local litter manufacturer offers $25 to any sitter who gets a pet store to stock his particular product. People trust you, so what could it hurt? Everything! Once anyone even suspects that you are getting financial rewards from a suggestion you make, your entire operation is suspect.

Never cloud your credibility by taking money for suggestions. Your money comes from pet sitting. That is your source of revenue. Once you firmly establish that you have no financial interest in any of your suggestions (from test products to charities) you will be respected for your stance. After all, if a customer switches to "brand X" because of your recommendation (and you are receiving gratuity for her choice) shouldn't it be your fault if it doesn't work?

I said very early in the book that your only job is pet sitting. You aren't the gardener, plant person, pool man, or the chauffeur. Any additional service that you add and charge for in your business diminishes your standing as a pet sitter. Your reputation can only be built on service. Service takes many forms other than just sitting for pets. Service is also suggestions, involvement in the community, and a genuine concern for your customer's needs.

Business is just Great!

Nothing succeeds like success is a phrase which must have been first uttered by someone who was successful. It is not an empty phrase. People enjoy doing business with successful people. Conversely, nobody willingly wishes to do business with a loser.

This correlation can be easily translated to your own business by following this rule:

When anybody asks you how your business would rate—you tell them your business is doing just great!

I don't care if you haven't had a booking in three weeks. Your business is doing just great. You never want to appear unsuccessful, even if you are in a slump.

I am constantly amazed, while making my rounds of pet shops, groomers, and veterinarians, how many of them admit to problems in business in answer to the question, "How's business?" I hear everything from thinking of selling, to wondering if the person is going to be able to meet the rent payments for the next month. Why do people say these things, even if they are apparently true? People don't stop to think of the impact it has on the listener. Here's a small scenario.

You are visiting with a veterinarian who asks you honestly how your business is going at present. Because you believe the inquiry to be a sincere question, you pour out your heart to the person. You tell the veterinarian that you really wish you had more business right now. Things are slow, not many calls are coming in, etc. You leave the office feeling much better having unburdened yourself of your immediate worries. But what really happened after you left?

You left that veterinarian with the lasting impression that your business was not good. When the next customer of the veterinarian picks up your card and asks the veterinarian for a recommendation, your vet may say something as simple as, "It's a good firm, but the business for them is rather slow right now, maybe you can help this firm out." Doesn't sound too bad, does it? Wrong, it is bad!

I don't want to do business with a loser. I want to do business with a successful person! I want a busy sitter who has lots of business. After all, a successful person equals a good person in many prospect's minds. If your business is slow, that may translate into you doing something wrong. After all, if you were doing everything right, your business would be good, wouldn't it?

The reverse of this situation is just as subliminally active. When a customer asks me to recommend a vet, groomer, or pet shop, I think back to those people who told me business was good. I automatically recommend those firms. Why? Because I want my customer to be happy with the choice, not burdened with a source whose business is in poor health.

If you always tell people you are busy, and you always tell people business is good, it will become a self-fulfilling prophecy.

If you must unburden your soul with your business worries, tell your problems to your spouse, relatives, or minister. Never let out an idle slip of the tongue which could have a negative impact on your business. When your business is *really* going well, then you just tell people that things are terrific!

Planning for the Future

Your business is thriving, money is rolling in, and your days are filled with jobs and activity, what else could you need? This might be a good time to look back and reflect on what you have accomplished and where you may have missed the mark.

If you have a spare wall in your office where you can put up a large map of your territory, here's what you do. Buy an inexpensive four-by-six-foot corkboard. Hang on the corkboard a map of your specific area. By some flags (pins) from your local stationery store which will serve as markers. You'll need four colors. Let's use red to represent merchants you visit who carry your cardholders. Green for the merchants who don't have your cardholders, but have agreed to pass along information about your service. Blue is for past and present customers, and finally yellow is for repeat (or year-round) customers.

Take the time to put a flag on the map for each of these four categories. You should have something over 100 flags sticking in the map. Sit down, pour yourself something hot and refreshing to drink, and stare at that map for a while. Ask yourself the following questions:

Are there some areas of my territory in which there are no flags? Why is that? Should I concentrate more on those areas?

Are there some areas of my territory in which I have many flags? Why is that? Is that an area I should concentrate on developing even further?

Are there some areas (cities) in which I have no business? Why is that? Do I have cards and literature out there?

Is there some area (outlying) in which I have little business but still advertise service? Should I consider dropping that area? (Time divided by driving costs = low profit.)

Is there a blank area that I really want to service where specific target advertising might help? (Direct mailing.)

Are my repeat (regular) customers in any one specific area? Why?

Is there a specific area in which a speaking engagement would help?

Is there an outlying area that is getting more and more customers where I should consider adding a person to the staff to cover it, instead of driving out there myself?

Is there an area of my territory in which I should consider raising my rates because of conditions? (Driving time, access, etc.?)

If I'm boarding birds, are they all coming from one certain area?

If you religiously stick flags into the map for every single business you deal with and customer you serve, you will soon see a pattern developing. You may be amazed when you first see a visual example of the area you cover. In my specific case, I was amazed to find that although I thought most of my customers were in one end of the territory, the majority of my customers were really in a different place altogether. What good did this information do me? For one thing, it taught me that I needed to raise my prices because I was facing a twenty-minute drive before I reached the area of my most active service.

Any graphic example you create can allow you to visualize your situation better. Charting out sales from month to month will soon teach you which months are better than others. A pattern starts to form which illustrates when to advertise, when to plan your own vacation, and where to spend your advertising dollars.

Considering the fact that 60 percent of households have pets, no one particular area should be any better than another for sitting possibilities. A good measure of this uniform spread of pets is to look through the yellow pages and see where the pet shops are located. Almost every city has at least two or three pet shops. All this means is that the possibilities for sitting assignments are not limited only to certain select areas. I know a lady who has thirty-nine sitters working for her in a city with less than 130,000 people. Imagine that! Yes, there are kennels in that city, too—five of them. Yes, the lady has competitors in the city too.

The lady has been in business for eight years and started just like you and me, doing every single sitting by herself.

A wise man once said, "You cannot know where you are going unless you know where you've been." Taking time out every three months to study what you've accomplished is a worthwhile activity.

One final thought on this subject. Keeping accurate records of your growth and development will be a great asset if and when you ever decide to sell your business. Just like service records on your car when selling to a private party, you can use your growth charts to illustrate where you started and how far you have come in customer development. It will help bolster, reinforce, and substantiate your selling price, proving to the prospective buyer that, indeed, you operate a viable, thriving business.

Award Notification Letter

(today's date)

Mrs. Irene Castoon
522 Paseo Del Mar
Palos Verdes Estates, California 90274

Dear Irene:

We are both pleased and proud to inform you that Fido and Rover Castoon have been selected as recipients of the first annual Paws Pronouncement Awards. They are our First Place Winners in the category of Best Overall Dogs. This category takes into account behavior, walking, discipline, attention, and affection.

Although this was admittedly a very partial decision on the part of the two judges, it was a competition from a field of over 200 other pets! These awards are very narrow in scope and encompass only one percent of our total client base served. You should be very proud of Fido and Rover.

In addition to the Certificate of Merit (enclosed) we are including a gift certificate for the winners which is worth $10 off any future sittings during the coming year of 199_.

Please give our best to both Fido and Rover on acceptance of this award which will last for the entire year of 199_.

Once again, congratulations for having two such great pets, and we look forward to being associated with them for a long time to come in the future.

Cordially,

Bill & Ellen Foster,
Owners/Sitters
PAW PARTNERS

Encls.

——————— *Your pet deserves the best.* ———————

The day is done, the game is through—
My friends and I rest, and wish the best to you.

20 What is the Best?

It was Oscar Wilde who quipped, "I am easily pleased. I am always satisfied with the best." There is a great confusion today between being number one and being the best. You can be the best and never even come close to being number one. Winning is not being the best, it is only winning. There are entrepreneurs in this world who start a business and make a million dollars a year, yet have expenses of $150 million per year! That's not winning or success, that's only failure.

Being the best in a service business is when you are recognized as being the best by customers, associates, and your own peer group. You are told you are the best. You perform like you are the best. Your service level is always ascending, not descending. You are always thinking up ways to improve your business. You continue to grow in your business, and give additional service over and above what is expected by the general public. That is being the best.

Being the best means doing each job as though it were for yourself, not the customer. You treat each job as though it were for your favorite relative, regardless of the money involved. Being the best is not dependent upon the weather, clients, stars, geography, season, or your own personal state of mind. Being the best is gained by being consistent and paying attention to detail.

When a customer tells me we did a good job, I am not happy. I want to hear we did more than was expected. I want the customer extremely pleased about our service. When I open each envelope containing a check from the customer, I am disappointed if there isn't a note inside telling us that we did a great job.

I expect every customer to be a repeat user of our service. I cannot imagine why anyone wouldn't use our service for the rest of their pet's lives, unless the family moved out of the area. Our repeat customer level is approaching 80 percent at this time and I won't be happy until it gets even higher. Being the best means expecting the best in every situation. How should this apply then to your business?

The physical aspect of being the best is simple enough. You start each job professionally and you do it to the best of your natural ability. You trust the customer will be pleased with the results. If the customer for any reason is not pleased, you immediately find out what is wrong and make every effort to correct the situation. Repetition in your work will streamline your operation until being the best comes easily and automatically to your daily habits. The only problem that may arise from trying to do the best possible job is when the health and safety of the pets conflict with owner's instructions. This can happen in some cases. Always opt for the health and safety of the pets, regardless of the owner's instructions. I would rather not be paid for a job (and know that I did the right thing) than collect money for endangering the welfare of the pets. Let's look at an example.

You have a two-day sitting job with a new customer. You enter the home and find the pet (in your opinion) in ill health. The dog appears listless, drooling at the mouth, anxious, and panic stricken. You take the dog to the veterinarian. The veterinarian diagnoses the pet as suffering from an acute anxiety attack brought on because of the owner's absence. (You later find out that the owner had not left the dog alone for eight years!) The dog gets a shot to calm him down and you finish the sitting. Two days later the owner returns and is upset with the $60 vet bill for what the owner considers an insufficient reason. The pet appears fine to the owner upon his return. The owner decides never to use your service again because of your arbitrary decision to take the dog to the vet, which cost the customer money. Was your decision wrong? No!

There will always be situations in which you cannot please everyone. What if you had not taken that dog to the vet? What if the dog had been physically ill and died? What would the owner's feelings toward you be in the event of the pet's death? What is the worst thing this person is going to say about your firm? Is this person going to say you are too cautious? You can live with that accusation. You cannot easily live with guilt. One last example from my own recent experience.

The owners left on a three-week European vacation. The large yard had a two-foot fence around the perimeter. The owners told us the dogs had jumped the fence in the past, but *probably* would stay in the yard if we let them run loose. We refused to do that. We kept the dogs on a leash at all times. The owners were somewhat unhappy upon returning to find that we hadn't let the dogs run free. Today I just got a call from those owners. Those same two dogs just jumped the fence and ran away. The owners hope that if I am in the area I may see them and return them. The owners now understand why we didn't let the dogs run free—but too late.

Being the best you can be is also a mental attitude. If you do not believe you are the best—you aren't. It is that simple. You cannot fool yourself into thinking you are something you are not. You either believe you are the best or you won't be the best. Being the best is not necessarily connected to a product. Being the best is in the attitude of the service you deliver.

Here's a brief test to prove to yourself that you can recognize the best right off the top of your head. Without giving the matter any deep thought, what place pops into your mind when you think about which, in your own opinion, is the best of these places?

the best gas station
the best restaurant
the best grocery store
the best pet shop
the best groomer
the best veterinarian.

Probably none of these six best places I just asked you about have national advertising, run commercials on television, give huge discounts, or are necessarily the lowest-priced places in town, are they? What makes them the best for you? People! You like the attitude, the friendliness, the atmosphere, the smile, the cheerfulness, the recognition, the familiarity, and the routine. You like those six places because you like the people who work in or own those places. They are the best for you not because radio or television said they were good but because you said they were good. You tell your friends about these places because you like them. You naturally think your friends will like them too, and you make these businesses successful by becoming a repeat customer.

What is the Best?

If you sat an alien down at a table, put the Hope diamond and a dirt clod side by side and asked the alien which was the best, which would the alien pick? With no one to prejudice the opinion of that person, it is a gamble either way. The product is not inherently good by itself. The service you offer could be done by a robot if the technology were available. People make the difference. You make the difference. You are the best, not your company. People are the company.

You can make money by being smart. You can gain customers (at least once) by being clever. You can stay in business by being doggedly determined. You can only be the best by being genuine. There is no substitute for the best. Oscar Wilde was right.

There you have your new business in a nutshell. You need to read many portions of this text over and over again and make notes as to what items you need to further develop and custom tailor to your own specific needs.

As I said in the beginning of the book, all of the forms have been provided for you and can be used just as they are written in some cases. Some forms will be best if you rework them according to your own personal situation. You need to work totally in the context of this book. My mistakes along the route, having nothing for comparison, have lead to the decisions to use the right methods—which do work!

If you have reasonably good health, have access to transportation, and can talk to people in person and on the telephone, you too can have an income of $50,000 or more per year. The choice is yours to make.

You should know by now that this is not a hypothetical plan that may or may not work. I am making my living, at present, from this very program which I have developed. If I can do it, you can do it too! The only limitations are your imagination and the time and energy you can devote to the business.

Remember that the new firm you have just decided to christen is a small business in the truest sense of the word. It is a one-owner firm, operated by you. Your customers do not expect you to have slick advertising, smooth copy, fancy cards, or a flashy automobile. As I said earlier in the text, I have attempted to keep these forms and fliers simple, inexpensive, and above all homemade. Homemade in this era is becoming not only acceptable, but truly fashionable. Folks are learning that big business is not the answer for all needs. The small entrepreneurial business is in an age of flourish. Take advantage of this turn of events. Capitalize on the fact that you are a small, one-person business. Be honest with your customers in telling them that you cannot afford dazzling advertising because with the low rates you charge the profit just isn't there. You'll be amazed at how many people will admire your forthright manner and candid explanations.

After you've been in business for six months, write and let me know how you did with your own business. I am interested in your success and want to help you with questions when they arise. I look forward to hearing from you—and to your success!

Best of fortune,

Bill Foster
P.O. Box 4581
San Pedro, California 90731